Forgotten Battles and American Memory

Wessagusset, Braddock, Cowpens, Lake Erie, Fort Pillow, Burma

DOUGLAS SMOCK

Copyright © 2022 Douglas Smock
All rights reserved
First Edition

PAGE PUBLISHING
Conneaut Lake, PA

First originally published by Page Publishing 2022

ISBN 978-1-6624-7523-8 (pbk)
ISBN 978-1-6624-7524-5 (digital)

Printed in the United States of America

To my father and all the forgotten soldiers,
and to my brother Bob, who inspired me to write this book.

CONTENTS

Introduction vii
Notes xiii

Chapter 1: Myles Standish and the Lost Colony 1
Chapter 2: Young George Washington and Braddock's Defeat ... 18
Chapter 3: Daniel Morgan and Cowpens 47
Chapter 4: Oliver Hazard Perry and the Battle of Lake Erie 73
Chapter 5: Nathan Bedford Forrest and the Fort Pillow
            Massacre 92
Chapter 6: "Vinegar Joe" Stilwell and the Battle for Burma 124

Acknowledgments 185
Bibliography 189
General Sources 199
Index 201

INTRODUCTION

This book revives six little-known American battles that offer lessons still valuable today. I go beyond tactics and strategies to look at how the battles are remembered today through monuments, museums, biographies, and in some cases, popular culture. It's interesting to look at how we, as Americans, choose to remember—or not remember—specific historical events and key figures, which is why I tied each chapter to an individual to examine more fully.

Battles often are symbolically significant.

In an essay in the book *Realms of Memory*, French historian Antoine Prost wrote, "Before 1916, Verdun was certainly not a central element of French national memory, but after the war it was *the* central element." French forces mounted a successful resistance to German invasion at Verdun, the longest and deadliest battle of World War I. The battle advanced past Joan of Arc, Le Tricolore, and the Reims Cathedral in French national consciousness, at least in Prost's view.

In the United States, Gettysburg resonates as a place of tremendous sacrifice, bravery, and importance in our national soul. But are there also important lessons in seemingly obscure events or battles? Unless they are rallying cries, such as Pearl Harbor or the Alamo, we generally want to forget military defeats or embarrassments.

People who have suffered great loss want their sacrifices to be remembered. There is a renewed Chinese interest in World War II battles, even those fought against the Japanese by the Nationalist Party, then in power. The Chinese Communist Party long suppressed the memory of their rival's successes with American soldiers in reopening a military supply route called the Burma Road. Calls for remembrance by survivors triggered a changing view in China, and today there are statues of American and Chinese soldiers at major battle sites. "Today's generation knows very little about the Second World War. We don't fear dying; we fear being forgotten," said an older person interviewed for a 2005 Shanghai television documentary. In America, Blacks feel the same way about the sacrifices made by Black soldiers. The sentiment is echoed by Native Americans. Most Americans want the forgotten soldiers to be remembered in their families, not to glorify war, but to honor their service and sacrifices. This book is an attempt to bring a few of them back to life in their own words as much as possible.

The first chapter reports on a deadly ambush of the Massachusett tribe by Myles Standish in present-day North Weymouth, Massachusetts, which no one wants to acknowledge because of its brutality and the exposure of a very dark side of the Pilgrims. Ren Green and her son Thomas, two present-day leaders of the tribe, told me that much was taken from them, but what mattered most to them was that their history and memory were not erased. A rival tribe tried to do exactly that. It was the same tribe that helped spark the Myles Standish attack. The state of Massachusetts made an icon of Myles Standish, whose murder of Native Americans was long ignored even in the neighborhood where it took place. Through at least 2021, the Massachusetts flag and state seal showed Standish's arm brandishing a saber above the head of a Native American standing at peace. So a commission was appointed to explore alternative designs.

The issue of memory is different in a battle just east of Pittsburgh, where Native Americans obliterated a sophisticated British army led by General Edward Braddock in 1755. That battle needs to be remembered because it witnessed significant growth in twenty-three-year-old George Washington, whose early military career was a humiliating failure. There is no state or national park at the Braddock field; it is remembered instead through a statue of Washington in a blighted neighborhood and a museum built through the determined enterprise of a retired local attorney. The battle's beginning between French Marines and British grenadiers is marked only by a patch of weeds behind a car-dealership-turned-exhibition-space. America's first major steel mill swallowed up a big chunk of the battlefield. There are only rumors of the location of a trench where some four hundred British and American soldiers were buried.

There is also little memory of two battles that recall how our country's fate was tied to short-term citizen soldiers. We all know about the minutemen at Lexington and Concord. But there is also the story of the repeated calls for mobilization of local militia in northwestern Pennsylvania in 1813 to protect naval vessels being built from scratch on Lake Erie. Those ships captured an entire Royal Navy squadron. There's a large monument and a museum commemorating the battle in Ohio, but its most powerful testimony are the old cemeteries almost invisible in the backwoods of northwestern Pennsylvania where hundreds of graves are festooned with War of 1812 markers topped with flags. Men as old as seventy were called to service, sometimes for just two or three weeks.

In another example of militia power, there was a significant overnight expansion of Daniel Morgan's undermanned army in Cowpens, South Carolina, in 1781 in what turned out to be a pivotal victory in the Revolutionary War. Local militias were detested by George Washington and his commanders. But the militia executed orders perfectly and helped engineer a rare double envelopment of an overeager British army. Part of the remembrance of the battle was the vilification of a British cavalry officer, an act perpetrated by "an American propaganda machine," in the opinion of one English writer. The story of Cowpens also shines light on a shameful episode of Black American history. The British "freed" slaves in 1775 if they would serve in their short-handed army. Many were labeled as British property and forced into menial labor. Most were returned to slavery, including a man and a woman taken from the British by American general Daniel Morgan after the battle. In 1783, George Washington asked a slave catcher in British-occupied New York City to track down six of his slaves who had escaped from Mount Vernon.

Remembrance is a major theme in my chapter on a little-known Civil War battle at Fort Pillow, Tennessee, where Confederate troops slaughtered Black soldiers after they had surrendered. The attackers were commanded by General Nathan Bedford Forrest, called "the Confederacy's greatest cavalryman" by one Southern historian. Novelist William Faulkner also loved Forrest even though he was a slave trader before the war and leader of the Ku Klux Klan after. Black leaders and activists are forcing a reckoning over how we remember Forrest and other Confederates. The heated back-and-forth about the meaning of historical symbols is a microcosm of the much-bigger political and social divide in our country today. The issue of how Southern Americans can honor their Confederate ancestors, who fought to maintain slavery, is a complicated controversy with no easy answer.

The stories offer lessons about command and control. Military discipline evaporated, resulting in slaughter at Braddock's Defeat, the Massacre at Fort Pillow in the Civil War, and the 1944 battle for Myitkyina in Burma. Daniel Morgan was in total control at the Battle of Cowpens and stopped a potential slaughter. Oliver Hazard Perry pulled out a victory in the Battle of Lake Erie despite gross insubordination by his second-in-command. George Washington's inability to control tribal allies became the opening volley of the Seven Years' War. There are also lessons in tactics. Joseph Stilwell adapted a British-developed concept of guerilla jungle warfare into an American-style maneuver of flanking and then attacking a surprised enemy. Morgan's double envelopment of the rapidly advancing British is still studied by the US Army.

Some of the stories in this book are personal to me. In 2013, I moved to a neighborhood south of Boston with a little park featuring a memorial garden to Native Americans. There was no explanation in the park of its significance, and my neighbors were mostly at a loss to explain it. That began a multiyear investigation into Myles Standish and an English trading colony that included discussions with two leaders of the modern-day Massachusett tribe.

I grew up in a town outside of Pittsburgh near Braddock's Defeat. Nothing was taught about the battle in my school, and very few people had any sense of what happened there. Three of my ancestors served in the Pennsylvania militia in 1813, defending Perry's vulnerable shipbuilding site. My father was a buck private muleskinner who described a horrific jungle march to the Burma Road in 1945. His letters home told of soldiers with typhus and broken legs who had to be tied to mules as they climbed up and down mountains.

I spent my career as a newspaper reporter and magazine editor and tried to approach each chapter as a story I researched, not as an academic investigation. I began with no goal to unearth never-reported-before research materials. Deep digging into original materials, however, did discover that a copy of a 1633 map of the Massachusetts Bay Colony in the British Library was different from the same map marked up by Charles Francis Adams Jr. that had been used for decades by local historians. My interpretation of the running battle between Standish and Massachusett warriors is unique, based on my research. I also discovered 1813 pay records in the Library of Congress for the Pennsylvania militia. Seeing one of the shallow-draft bateau in the Fort LeBoeuf Museum in Waterford, Pennsylvania, helped me understand how fast-moving French Marines traversed a shallow creek I had explored as a child in the 1950s. Access to online resources was a critical help during the coronavirus pandemic of 2020 and 2021. Many records and diaries are now available online. They include the digitized diaries of Burma leaders Stilwell and Ernest Easterbrook in the Hoover Archives at Stanford University. The George C. Marshall Research Library in Lexington, Virginia, is also a treasure trove of valuable documents I was able to explore in person.

"War is a human tragedy, but the memory of war becomes a resource for humankind," Chinese scholar Zhou Yong told British historian Rana Mitter while explaining his study of the wartime destruction of Chongqing. "The war years in Chongqing created a new moral universe for China," Mitter wrote in *China's Good War: How World War II Is Shaping a New Nationalism*.

Doug Smock
North Weymouth, Massachusetts
October 2021

NOTES

In some cases, the estimates of troop strength listed in the "orders of battle" for each chapter are highly contested, particularly since commanders often inflated the strength of their opponents and underestimated their own strength. My efforts to identify accurate troop strengths included a study of battle reports, pension records, and analyses by leading historians as well as other third-party sources. Sometimes, estimates vary wildly, such as for Daniel Morgan's troop strength at the Battle of Cowpens. No one counted the number of Native Americans who attacked Braddock's army in 1755. In those cases, I used my best estimate, a range, or a number with a plus sign. For the Battle for the Burma Road, I used authorized Army troop strengths because of convalescents or medical evacuees. Those numbers are supplemented with an actual troop count taken during the battle for the 475th Regiment as recorded in Colonel Ernest Easterbrook's diary at the Hoover Institution. Troop strength issues are discussed in the text as needed.

With names, I used versions most familiar to Westerners. So in chapter 1, it's *Plymouth Plantation* instead of *Plimoth*. It's *Myles Standish* instead of *Miles*. But the name of the tourist attraction in Plymouth, Massachusetts, is Plimoth-Patuxet. And it's "The Courtship of Miles Standish" because that's the name of the poem. Native American names are even more confusing because contemporary English writers rendered names very differently. Where possible, I deferred to versions used by tribes today, such as the Massachusett and Wampanoag. There's confusion because English writing in seventeenth-century colonial America was generally phonetic, and the Native American language was oral.

In chapter 6, I use Chinese names as they were known in the West during the 1940s, such as Mao Tse-tung. In the mid-1950s, China adopted an improved system for Westernizing Mandarin called pinyin. That system was widely adopted in the West following the normalization of relations with China. So Mao became *Mao Zedong*. The pinyin names are in parentheses in my text when first mentioned. To be consistent, I indicated Chiang Kai-shek's pinyin name although Taiwan did not formally adopt the system. Also, in chapter 6, I use Japanese names as they are known today. Starting around 2008, the family name goes after the given name when written in English.

CHAPTER 1

Myles Standish and the Lost Colony

> *Mr. Weston's colony had by their evil and debauched courage so exasperated the Indians among them… But their treachery was discovered unto us, and we went to rescue the lives of our countrymen and take vengeance on them for their villainy.*
>
> —Governor William Bradford,
> Plymouth Plantation

Myles Standish is an icon of colonial American history. He represents leadership, security, and even romanticism, as he was fondly remembered by Henry Wadsworth Longfellow in "The Courtship of Miles Standish." The poem, written in 1858, was largely myth, but Longfellow defended its veracity, saying the stories were handed down by his family, including the two *Mayflower* descendants featured in a love triangle with Standish.

Yet he led an ambush of Native American braves who might have constituted a threat, beheaded at least one of them, and then impaled the head on the stockade fence surrounding Plymouth Plantation. It was a stark, and effective, warning to other tribes in the area.

The Massachusetts State seal depicts Myles Standish's saber hovering above a Native American at rest. A commission was appointed in 2021 to develop a new seal.

Massachusetts chose to recognize Standish in its state flag and seal, which depicts an arm brandishing a saber above a Native American resting at peace. The appropriateness of the symbology was not officially questioned until January 2021, when Governor Charlie Baker appointed a committee to develop a replacement. There are many other tributes to Standish in Massachusetts. A sculpture by Daniel Chester French of six characters from Longfellow's poems, including Standish, is located in Cambridge. A state forest was named in his honor. A statue of Standish rests on a 116-foot tower in Duxbury. Even a dormitory used by Boston University was named in his honor.

No incident demonstrates the inappropriateness of the Standish mythology more than the attack led by Standish on the two braves.

In March 1623, leaders of the struggling Plymouth Plantation dispatched Standish, their paid military leader, to a coastal settlement twenty-five miles north with a savage mandate: return with the head of a warrior named Wituwamat.

He was the perceived leader of a rumored multitribal strike against a failed English trading post and possibly Plymouth itself. With a handful of men and a Native ally named Hobbamock, Standish ambushed Wituwamat, a powerful brave named Pecksuot, and two other Natives in a locked room and then engaged in a running battle with another group of warriors in present-day North Weymouth, Massachusetts.

They were joined by a few members of the trading colony established a year earlier by London investor Thomas Weston and his merchant "Adventurer" partners to capitalize on the profitable beaver trade with the Massachusett tribe. A few days later, Wituwamat's head was proudly impaled on the stockade at the entrance to Plymouth Plantation—a warning to the local Native populations. It was an important moment in American history, and a largely forgotten one.

The attack clearly established the primacy of the Pilgrims. The local tribes that had quarreled with the new English settlers quickly dissipated, clearing the way for a massive Puritan migration to the Massachusetts Bay Colony, anchored at Boston.

The Natives feared the Pilgrims' guns, their ruthlessness, and their rumored ability to unleash a deadly plague on command. The violent, preemptive strike was condemned even by the Pilgrims' own spiritual leader, John Robinson, who had remained at their safe haven in Holland.

The necessity of the strike is still debated. America prefers to remember the banquet between the Pilgrims and the local Natives, formally proclaimed as Thanksgiving by President Abraham Lincoln in 1863. There was indeed a feast, albeit a strained affair, between the Pilgrims and a group of Natives, called the Pokanoket Wampanoags, who had sought a military alliance to stave off possible annihilation by the rival Narragansett tribe, located in present-day Rhode Island.

The story of how tensions escalated to the murder and decapitation of Wituwamat began with the arrival of the first Europeans. Giovanni da Verrazzano, a Florentine, was hired by French merchants to search the area from Florida to Newfoundland for a passage to Asia. He discovered Cape Cod Bay in 1524. In 1605, English captain George Weymouth kidnapped five friendly Abenaki Natives while exploring the coast of Maine. They were viewed as valuable sources of intelligence by investor groups in England anxious for information. One of their jailers and inquisitors in England was Sir Ferdinando Gorges, who two years later joined Thomas Weston and other investors in establishing a short-lived trading colony in Maine.

Captain John Smith, of Jamestown fame, explored the region in 1614 with several vessels. One of his commanders, Thomas Hunt, captured twenty-seven Wampanoag Natives and sold them into slavery in Málaga, Spain. That action negatively affected English and Native relations for years to come, in Smith's view. Native Americans, and not Africans, were the first people enslaved by Europeans in this country. One of those captured was a brave named Squanto, who later returned. The first Europeans spread infectious diseases that obliterated some coastal populations, including a village called Patuxet, which had been Squanto's home.

In 1615, the Natives took revenge on a wrecked French ship, killing most of the sailors and keeping a few as slaves. One of the Natives participating in the butchery was Pecksuot, who later taunted Weston colonists and Standish with his gruesome account.

English sailors then continued the butchery, reportedly murdering several members of the Wampanoags, who responded by attacking a party led by an explorer and gold prospector named Thomas Dermer. In his best-selling book titled *Mayflower*, Nathaniel Philbrick wrote, "When the Mayflower arrived at Provincetown Harbor in November, it was generally assumed by the Indians that the ship had been sent to avenge the attack on Dermer. In the weeks ahead, the Pilgrims did little to change that assumption."

Weston and Gorges were key figures in organizing the Pilgrims' trip. Weston fronted a group of English merchants, some of whom belonged to a speculative investment group called the Merchant Adventurers. He heard of the Pilgrims' interest in establishing a colony and traveled to Holland to pitch himself. He connected them to Gorges, who had a royal patent, or permit, to settle in the northern part of the Virginia claim, which extended to the Hudson River.

Terms of the arrangement were dramatically changed by Weston at the last minute, upsetting the Pilgrims. In one of the changes, the investors insisted on including a handpicked group of men, such as Stephen Hopkins, who had been part of the Jamestown Colony. The Pilgrims, with little choice, accepted the newly imposed conditions. They headed for America and were blown off course and landed in present-day Provincetown, Massachusetts, on November 11, 1620.

A Pilgrim landing party raided a buried supply of corn seed, ripped through a grave site, and was chased off a beach under a hail of arrows. The scouting party, sailing up the coast, found a spot with a harbor, fresh water, and a hill for a fort, and started to build homes. It was the site of Patuxet, the village that had been wiped out by disease.

The settlement at Plymouth was poorly provisioned, and 52 of the 102 who had arrived on Cape Cod were dead by spring. Squanto, who had learned to speak English, befriended the Pilgrims and helped establish a treaty with Massasoit Ousamequin of the Pokanoket Wampanoags. But Corbitant, a leader of the Pocasset tribe of the Wampanoag, challenged Massasoit's treaty with the Pilgrims. The treaty seemed like a straightforward military alliance but actually undercut long-standing tribal legal tradition, according to Paula Peters, a present-day activist for the Mashpee Wampanoag tribe.[1]

Standish was dispatched to a village called Namasket with fewer than a dozen men to kill and behead Corbitant, who escaped. Later, the Narragansetts, also unhappy with the Pilgrims, sent Plymouth Plantation a bundle of arrows wrapped in a snakeskin, a threat.

---

[1] Paula Peters, "A Man without a Tribe: The True Story of Squanto," *The Patriot Ledger*, Quincy, Massachusetts, November 24, 2020.

Standish ordered construction of a palisade fence surrounding their homes and beefed up other fortifications.

Meanwhile, the Pilgrims were struggling to feed themselves, let alone return a profit to the London investment group that had paid their way. An initial plan to farm communally was an abject failure, and only twenty-six acres were planted in 1621. In 1623, each family was given permission to plant privately, with the amount of land determined by family size.[2]

"The Pilgrims, in their quest to be stepping-stones for freedom, had almost everything go wrong as they attempted to plant a colony in the new world. By the time they reached the shores of New England, they were poor, had barely enough provisions for the first winter, and began to die at an alarming rate," wrote Paul Jehle, executive director of the Plymouth Rock Foundation.

The *Mayflower* returned to London in 1621 empty of cargo. Weston was not happy. A return ship carried this message to Plymouth governor William Bradford: "The life of the business depends upon the lading of this ship, which if you do to any good purpose, that I may be freed from the great sums I have disbursed for the former and must do for the latter (the Fortune), I promise you I will never quit the business."

Despite his commitment, Weston bailed on the Plymouth investment and created another venture: a trading colony of some sixty men. No religious separatists this time. No women. No children. Just men, albeit a rough group, who would engage in the profitable beaver trade.

His traders arrived at Plymouth in the fall of 1622 poorly provisioned and not prepared to establish a settlement. They left for an area on the coast that the Natives called Wessaguscus and they called Wessagusset. They were greeted by the local Massachusett leader Aberdikes, who welcomed the idea of trade. But the situation soon deteriorated.

The alert of an emerging crisis came from a man named Phineas Pratt, a member of the Weston Colony at Wessagusset, who chronicled his story in 1664 when he petitioned the colonial government

---

[2] Paul Jehle, "Economic Liberty in America: A Legacy of the Pilgrim," Chalcedon.edu, January 5, 2014, https://chalcedon.edu/magazine/economic-liberty-in-america-a-legacy-of-the-pilgrims.

for the financial benefits accorded firstcomers. He was the only Weston colonist to make a written record.

Pratt's account went like this: When the Weston party of sixty men arrived at Wessagusset in 1622, "there was a great plague among the savages and, as themselves told us, half their people died thereof… The savages seemed to be good friends with us while they feared us, but when they saw famine prevail, they began to insult."

Pecksuot sought to intimidate the newcomers with boasts of how the tribe had subdued the shipwrecked French crew. "We made them our servants. They wept much… We took away their clothes. They lived but a little while."

Later, Aberdikes approached the colony with several armed braves and accused one of the men of stealing corn. They retreated when they saw men armed with muskets behind a fence palisade surrounding three structures. According to legend, the Weston colonists hung a proxy for the crime, an older man who was deathly ill.

The colonists buttoned up the palisade and consumed what food they had left while braves watched. Pratt continued, "When we understood that their plot was to kill all English people in one day when the snow was gone, I would have sent a man to Plymouth, but none were willing to go. Then I said if Plymouth men know not of this treacherous plot, they & we are all dead men; therefore, if God willing, tomorrow I will go."

Pratt made a successful escape to Plymouth, where he found preparations already underway for a small military expedition to Wessagusset. Edward Winslow had just arrived after a medical healing mission to Massasoit, and he told of a multitribal plan to attack Plymouth and the Weston Colony.

Spurred by the warning of Massasoit and later confirmed by Pratt, the Pilgrims sent Standish to ambush the tribal leaders. They took a small vessel called a shallop and arrived on March 26, 1623, at Wessagusset, where the colony's ship, the *Swan*, was anchored. No one was on board, and Standish fired a musket. Several men suddenly appeared. Surprised to find Standish, they said there was no imminent threat from the tribe and that, in fact, some of the colonists were cohabitating with them.

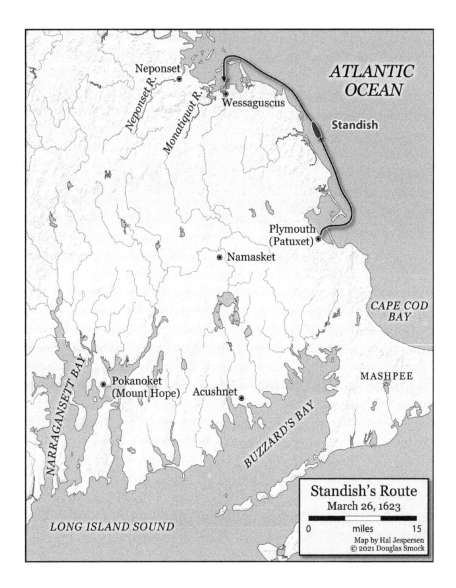

The Plymouth militia sailed to Wessaguscus in a small vessel called a shallop that had been used to explore the coast after the arrival of the Mayflower. The trip was delayed by bad weather after the assassination of an elite Massachusett brave named Wituwamat was approved by a three-person council.

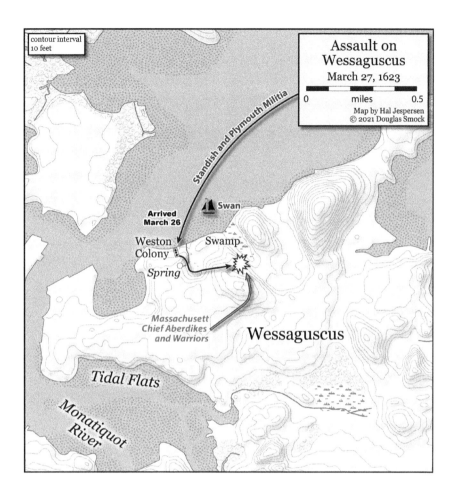

This map shows placement of Weston Colony roughly equivalent to a location shown by Massachusetts Bay Colony governor John Winthrop, who visited the site in the early 1630s. The exact location of the colony has been debated since the nineteenth century. The site of the running battle is the estimate of the author.

Standish collected colonists in their hilltop stockade and told them of his plan to lure Natives inside and then kill them. The Natives perceived the threat, and only Wituwamat, Pecksuot, and two other men ventured into the small fort. Standish promised them a feast and invited them into a house. He then locked the door, grabbed

Pecksuot's knife, and killed him. Then his other soldiers killed and decapitated Wituwamat. A third brave was hanged.

Assault on Wessaguscus
Order of Battle

Plymouth Plantation and Weston Colony
10 to 14 combatants
Captain Myles Standish
Hobomock, Pokanoket Wampanoag pniese, or elite warrior
Eight unnamed members of the Plymouth militia
Three or four Weston colonists

Massachusett Tribe
Probably 8 to 30 combatants
Described as a "file" in a report of the battle
Chief Aberdikes (also known as Octabiest, and probably Chickataubut)
Unknown number of warriors

Aberdikes approached with warriors, and the conflict debouched into a running battle in the surrounding area. The Natives, outgunned, disappeared into the tall cattails of a marsh. At the end of the day, seven Natives were killed. No English died in combat. The settlement was evacuated, with most colonists sailing the *Swan* to a fishing outpost in Maine.

Accounts of Standish's attack came from Edward Winslow, of Plymouth Plantation, in a detailed report to London titled *Good Newes From New England*. Accounts were also provided by Bradford (*Of Plymouth Plantation*) and Thomas Morton (*The New English Canaan*). Winslow was the de facto agent with Massasoit, as well as with the investors who had funded the Pilgrims' trip.

Most of the local tribes fled the area, fearing another attack. Bradford lamented the lost ability to profit from further beaver fur trade—at least for a while. The peace that prevailed in the area was short-lived. Massasoit's son Metacom planned to continue friendly relations with the English and took the name of Philip. But tensions over land use and diminished game erupted in the 1670s, leading to an armed conflict called King Philip's War. Colonial militia overwhelmed the tribal coalition, and there was slaughter on both sides. Metacom was killed by militia in 1676.

Events at the Weston Colony were later mythologized in Longfellow's 1858 narrative poem "The Courtship of Miles Standish." Samuel Butler recalled the proxy hanging in his satirical poem titled "Hudibras," published in the mid-seventeenth century.

Longfellow wasn't the only *Mayflower* descendant who distorted or soft-pedaled history. Meetings held by the Alden Kindred of America aren't likely to review the sophisticated .5-caliber Italian-made wheel-lock carbine that John Alden's descendants donated to the National Rifle Association's Firearms Museum at its headquarters in Fairfax, Virginia. Ric Burns, who included tough-to-watch scenes of Wituwamat's head at Plymouth Plantation in a 2015 PBS *American Experience* documentary, became persona non grata at the General Society of *Mayflower* Descendants.[3] These groups are often more interested in the embellishment of their ancestors than in current scholarship, or even the facts in some cases.

The tribes have a modest presence in Massachusetts today. The Wampanoags, led in part by Paula Peters, made a failed bid (as of 2021) for a federal casino license. The Massachusett tribe is greatly diminished, but one group still holds tribal meetings not far from their ancestral home in the Blue Hills area near Boston. They were confined "for their protection" in 1657 in a reservation called Ponkapoag in present-day Canton, Massachusetts, southwest of Boston. Today, the headquarters of Dunkin Donuts (now Dunkin') towers over the northern edge of the old reservation land.

---

[3] Walter Powell, executive director of the General Society of *Mayflower* Descendants (2013–2017), comment made to author, July 11, 2021.

After the Ponkapoag site gradually disappeared, many members moved to segregated areas, such as Indian Row in Brockton, Massachusetts.[4] In the 2010 census, just eighty-five people identified as Ponkapoag Massachusett.

Thomas Green, left, and his mother, Ren Green, maintain the tradition of the Massachusett tribe, but their numbers are dwindling.

Tension between the tribes continued into the twenty-first century. Brenda "Ren" Green, one of the sachems, or leaders, of the Ponkapoag Massachusett, challenged Paula Peters, of the Wampanoags, in a standing-room-only meeting at the Weymouth Public Library when Peters claimed the Wampanoags' territory had included the Blue Hills area of Boston.[5] The presentation was part of

---

[4] Brenda Green, Massachusett sachem, comment made to author, Moswetuset Hummock in Quincy, Massachusetts, June 2015.

[5] Comments made at a meeting in April 2015 at the Tufts Library in Weymouth, Massachusetts.

a promotion for Plymouth 400, a commemoration of the four hundredth anniversary of the founding of Plymouth Plantation.

It was an attempt, said Green, to claim the Boston area site for a casino. Peters said it was a misunderstanding. Speaking generally, Walter Powell, a historian and chair of the historical committee of Plymouth 400 at the time of the presentation, wrote to me in 2021, saying, "I was not too surprised (but often frustrated) by the degree to which local politics and personalities also influence (and sometimes complicate) our 'understanding' of the events of 1620 and afterward." Powell's perspective also includes thirty-five years of battlefield preservation and local government involvement in Gettysburg, Pennsylvania.

Green and her son Thomas, currently the vice president of the Massachusett-Ponkapoag Tribal Council, still work to maintain the traditions and memory of their ancestors.[6] In 2015, members of the Massachusett tribe spoke at a dedication of the newly restored Moswetuset Hummock in Quincy, Massachusetts, which had been used as a summer seat by the tribe in the 1620s.

Today, on some days, you can talk to an actor portraying Phineas Pratt at Plimoth Patuxet, the name of the popular tourist site recreating the Plymouth Colony and a reimagined adjacent Wampanoag camp. On a sunny spring day, I found a youthful Pratt working a field at the bottom of a hill. He was surprised and excited that someone wanted to speak with him. He was particularly surprised that I lived in Wessagusset, which is still dealing with its odd place in history. Yes, he told me, he had arrived at Plymouth from Wessagusset. Yes, he had escaped the troubles and alerted the colonists. Yes, Wituwamat's head was spiked and stank in the sun.

Plymouth Plantation is commemorated at Plymouth Patuxet and at historical sites in the town of Plymouth. A recent high-tech archaeological dig by the University of Massachusetts–Boston identified the hilltop site of a palisade wall that protected the settlement.

The Weston Colony site is another matter. It disintegrated not too long after Standish and his soldiers departed on their shallop. Per

---

[6] Thomas and Brenda Green were interviewed by the author in June 2015.

local tradition in the mid-nineteenth century, the site was located near a freshwater creek feeding into a cove in what today is called the Fore River. That view changed in 1884, when a map created in 1633 or 1634 by Governor John Winthrop of the Massachusetts Bay Colony was noticed in the British Museum by a person who understood its possible significance to early American history.

It showed three structures near a cove where the Fore River opens to what is now called Hingham Bay. It was labeled Wessaguscus.

It was conventional wisdom for more than one hundred years that the Weston Colony in Weymouth, Massachusetts, was located on a small hilly peninsula located in front of the houses in this photo. The peninsula was removed in the 1890s for fill used to build a marine terminal in South Boston. Now, other nearby sites are being considered

Historian Charles Francis Adams Jr., a descendant of two presidents, did a deep dive into the issue in the 1880s armed with the Winthrop map, a few descriptions of the topography in the Phineas Pratt account, and a dollop of common sense. It seemed obvious to Adams that the Weston Colony fort was best located on a hill that offered views of the bay and the mouth of the river. It needed a source of fresh water. There was a hill on a hook of land jutting into a cove next to the houses on the Winthrop map. There was a spring and a swamp nearby that could have been the one mentioned by Pratt. Adams was convinced this site, called Hunt's Hill, was the location of the Weston Colony.

His logic is still the generally accepted wisdom. In the early 1890s, a salvage company was looking for fill for a large marine park being built in South Boston. The hill on the cove was for sale. Adams strenuously objected, but the hill was sold with no effort at archaeological excavation.

Today a group called the Plymouth Archaeological Rediscovery Project is having second thoughts about the Hunt's Hill site. Its director, an archaeologist named Craig Chartier, said the Winthrop map possibly could have identified buildings built after the Weston Colony was abandoned. He identified four other sites in the immediate area as possibilities. One of them is near the creek on the Fore River. Another one, though, called the Bicknell site, is particularly interesting.

It meets the key criteria: hilltop, ocean frontage, freshwater access, and a nearby swamp, as described by Phineas Pratt. Two sets of human remains were discovered near the Bicknell site when houses were built. A Weymouth historian named G. Stinson Lord reported in a commemorative book in 1972 that seven bodies were found at one grave site and two decapitated bodies were found in another.[7]

In 2009, an archeological dig commissioned by the Weymouth Historical Commission was launched at the site (43 Bicknell Road, Weymouth) where the seven bodies were found. An early owner of the house (or their contractors) had placed four of the skulls in the foundation of the house. Looming at the crest of a hill like something out of an Alfred Hitchcock novel, the place is known to a handful of people as the House of Skulls. One occupant claimed the ghost of Pecksuot haunted the house.

---

[7] G. Stinson Lord and Jack Frost, *Two Forts...to Destiny* (North Scituate, Massachusetts: Hawthorne Press, 1972), 75.

The dig found nothing in or around the house. Did that really mean anything? If the colonists had left some metal tableware or knives behind, wouldn't they have been quickly scooped up by the Natives?

Archaeologist Chartier tried to stir up interest in another dig in a different location as the COVID-19 pandemic eased in 2021. There wasn't much appetite for any further exploration. One local historical activist said, "I think we should let those lost souls rest in peace."

While there are no physical remains of the Weston colony, there are lingering issues. There is a strong feeling, for example, that the stories of Native Americans in the area need to be better represented. For example, the living history exhibit at Plymouth dropped the word *plantation* in 2020 and replaced it with the word *Patuxet*, with plans to improve an adjacent Wampanoag site. Massachusetts decided it needed a new state seal.

The Wessagussett Memorial Garden was built with private funds in a small municipal park in the general location of the lost Weston Colony in Weymouth, Massachusetts.

In 1999, a Weymouth town meeting voted to purchase a tract of land near the House of Skulls in Wessagusset for conservation and historical purposes. A memorial garden, built with private funds raised by local resident Jodi Purdy, a descendant of Myles Standish, commemorates Massachusett Natives killed by the colonists. Another memorial was then installed nearby by descendants of John Sanders, the second governor of the Weston Colony. An area of infrequently mowed grass leads back toward the House of Skulls.

One of the Native American memorials in the park reads, "On October 21, 2001, these puddingstone memorials were dedicated as symbols of hope that the souls of the first inhabitants of Wessagusset, the Massachusett Indians, and the first settlers of Weymouth, the Weston colonists, have reconciled their differences and found peace."

I started an effort in 2018 to place a town historical marker at the park. The proposal was approved, and in October 2021, three historical markers were placed in the park, including one on the Massachusett tribe. At the dedication ceremony, Thomas Green, after starting with a greeting in native Algonquin language, said, "I am Spirit Creek of the Massachusett tribe. We are here today to bring to light the horrific treachery the English colonists brought to our ancestors in this place almost four hundred years ago. We are here to bring to light the willingness of those colonists' descendants to recognize and endeavor to atone for those transgressions. We commend our neighbors in Weymouth for accepting the truth of this sordid past and their continued effort to work with and learn from the indigenous stewards of this land, the enduring Massachusett tribe."

CHAPTER 2

Young George Washington and Braddock's Defeat

These savages may indeed be a formidable Enemy to your raw American Militia; but upon the King's Regular and disciplin'd Troops, Sir, it is impossible that they should make any Impression.

—General Edward Braddock,
to Benjamin Franklin

The dastardly behavior of the English Soldiers exposed all those who were inclined to do their duty to almost certain death...at length, in despite every effort to the contrary, broke and ran as sheep before the hounds.

—George Washington,
twenty-three-year-old aide-de-camp to Braddock

The annihilation of a British army by Native Americans and a small number of French soldiers in the southwestern Pennsylvania wilderness in 1755 was a turning point in the nascent development of a twenty-three-year-old George Washington. Today a statue of Washington that shines brightly gold in sunlight marks the spot near where Washington unsuccessfully urged British major general Edward Braddock to fight the warriors wilderness-style. The statue is surrounded by urban blight. America's oldest operating steel mill occupies part of the battlefield.

America loves its battlefields, but not this one. More than a dozen Civil War battlefields are virtual national shrines to the heroes and the fallen, but at Braddock's Field, there are no helpful National Park Service or American Battlefield Trust markers. A state historical sign located near the Washington statue was misplaced for more than thirty years in an adjacent town. It's an odd example of how we remember, or choose not to remember, history in the United States.

The Battle of the Monongahela (or Braddock's Defeat), fought on July 9, 1755, is important because it was a testing ground for George Washington, who stood tall while the British were slaughtered and ran. He and other Americans, such as Benjamin Franklin, took note that the seemingly invincible British Army was vulnerable.

In the first major engagement of the French and Indian War, a regular British army led by Major General Edward Braddock was crushed by a small force of French Canadian Marines and about 650 Native Americans who had to be cajoled into the fight. It was probably the most stunning battle ever won by North America's indigenous peoples. The number of Braddock's soldiers killed exceeded Custer's losses at Little Bighorn. Braddock's Defeat was one of the biggest military upsets since three Roman legions were obliterated by German tribes in the Battle of the Teutoburg Forest in AD 9. The casualty rate for Braddock's army was 60 percent, one of the highest ever recorded. The casualty rate for officers lieutenant and above was 70 percent. As a comparison, not quite one-third of the soldiers engaged at Gettysburg were casualties.

A museum at the site was founded by a retired attorney named Robert Messner, who housed artifacts in a refurbished building once owned by a Pontiac dealer. Weeds out back mark the site where British grenadiers confronted an onward-rushing column of French who had recently arrived in a hurried trip from Montreal to defend a new French fort at the source of the Ohio River (often called Forks of the Ohio). The site of present-day Pittsburgh, it was a very strategic and highly coveted location.

The battle is a study of a sudden turn of events, fratricide (intentional and unintentional killing of one's own forces), and poor tactical decisions on the part of Braddock and other officers. British hubris, firepower, numerical superiority, and organization were totally unhinged by a stealthy, disorganized, and terrifying opponent. Amid the chaos, Washington displayed the patience, competence, and presence under fire that would become his hallmark.

Braddock's Defeat, although striking, was not historically significant. The British simply redoubled efforts to overwhelm a lightly manned French outpost and dispatched another, bigger army, led by General John Forbes. The French were swept from the area within three years.

The battle was significant because of its impact on Washington, who matured under fire and saw that a highly trained and well-armed British army could be defeated. Benjamin Franklin, who had been helpful in supporting Braddock's expedition, noted in his autobiography, "This whole Transaction gave us Americans the first Suspicion that our exalted Ideas of the Prowess of British Regulars had not been well founded."

The battle was an early American front in a broader contest between the English, French, and other nations for multicontinent supremacy in what was termed the Seven Years' War in Europe and the French and Indian War in America.

In the early 1750s, the English and the French both coveted the Ohio Valley, which included tributaries stretching almost to Lake Erie. In 1752, French king Louis XV dispatched a tough-minded naval officer named Michel-Ange Duquesne de Menneville to New France to shore up French fur trading interests. He evicted British merchants, improved relations with Native tribes, and built forts along water routes: Fort de la Presqu'île, Fort de la Rivière au Bœuf (or LeBoeuf), Fort Machault, and a fort named after him at the Forks of the Ohio. The French claimed the area based on explorations by La Salle in the seventeenth century.

In August 1753, English king George II told Virginia governor Robert Dinwiddie to deliver an ultimatum to the French to vacate newly built forts. Dinwiddie also had a private commercial interest in evicting the French; he was an investor in the Ohio Company, which had been formed in 1748 to explore and develop the promising region. Lawrence Washington, George's older brother, was also an investor.

The British Crown granted the Ohio Company some of the territory but required it to build a fort and to settle one hundred families within seven years. It was an auspicious moment for Washington. His brother Lawrence had just died from tuberculosis, and his part-time post commanding the Virginia militia was vacated. George Washington made his interest in the command known to Dinwiddie, who appointed Washington a district adjutant of the militia.

Washington, at the age of twenty-one, was appointed to deliver the eviction directive to the French. He recruited six Virginians to go with him, including backwoodsman Christopher Gist to serve as guide. They set out on an old trail through the Allegheny Mountains in early winter, stopping for rest at the riverside cabin of a trader named John Fraser, whose trading post farther north had been taken over by the French. Washington investigated the nearby Forks of the Ohio as a possible fort location. He noted that it was "extremely well situated for a fort, as it has the absolute command of both rivers."

Along the way, Washington met with Native Americans in an effort to gain their support. One of them was Tanaghrisson, who was called Half King by the English. He was an Ohio Iroquois and nominally an ally of the English. French officers fed Washington dinner at Fort LeBoeuf and informed him they would not leave.

When Washington returned to Virginia, he was given the rank of lieutenant colonel by Dinwiddie and told to raise a militia. The young officer was dismissive of his new recruits, calling them "loose, idle persons." Complaints about local militia would become a common refrain later in his career. Meanwhile, a small group of Virginia fur traders was building a fort at the Forks of the Ohio on Dinwiddie's orders. A French Canadian force of one thousand, arriving by water, stopped the work quickly and built their own fort, which they named after Duquesne.

Washington heard the news while on a road-building mission on the way to southwestern Pennsylvania with his newly formed militia company of about 150 men. The French dispatched an ensign named Joseph Coulon de Villiers, Sieur de Jumonville, and thirty men to find Washington and deliver a note demanding that the Virginians and English stay out of French-claimed territory.

Not knowing he was being pursued by a diplomatic mission, Washington established camp at a place called Great Meadows, a glacial field located a little more than fifty miles south of Fort Duquesne. The camp included a crude structure just fourteen feet square built to store gunpowder, cornmeal, and other supplies. It was surrounded by a small white oak palisade. Half King and a complement of braves told Washington that about thirty-five French soldiers were camped at a boulder-studded glen nearby.

Washington's party of forty surprised the French, killing ten, including their leader, who was carrying diplomatic papers. According to a French account, Jumonville was brutally murdered while reading the ultimatum. It isn't clear what happened at the glen, but even in Washington's account, he lost control of his Native allies and the dead French were scalped. Not surprisingly, the Virginians, French, and Native Americans presented starkly different versions of who did what.[8]

Even before the incident, the area was a tinderbox that threatened to ignite a global conflagration because of already-existing tensions in Europe involving multiple countries. It is often said that the killing of Jumonville was the spark that ignited the Seven Years' War. Voltaire wrote in 1756, "So complicated are the political interests of the present times, that a shot fired in America shall be the signal for setting all Europe together by the ears." Of course, any number of incidents could have triggered war between England, France, and other countries.

At that time, a more mature officer would have headed back to Virginia, but Washington ordered his troops to build breastworks at Great Meadows. Called Fort Necessity, it was a poor choice for

---

[8] David Preston, "When Young George Washington Started a War," *Smithsonian* (October 2019).

a defensive position. The meadows were boggy and surrounded by trees on low hills. Sensing impending doom, Half King and his warriors left.

The French were out for blood and sent a six-hundred- to seven-hundred-soldier force, commanded by Jumonville's older brother, that included Native warriors to defeat Washington, who received reinforcements of British colonial regulars from South Carolina commanded by an officer with higher rank than Washington. So there also were command issues at the fort.

In early July 1754, the French overwhelmed the pathetic Fort Necessity. As a condition of surrender, Jumonville demanded Washington sign a document in French calling his brother's death an assassination. He signed it and returned, humiliated, to Virginia. Washington later maintained that his translator said the French word in the document, *assasinat*, meant "loss" or "death of." Either way, he had no choice but to accept the surrender. The French had won the first major propaganda victory of the war. It was the only time in Washington's career that he surrendered his troops.

After reading Washington's captured journal, Duquesne wrote, "Nothing could be more shameful, so base or so black as the train of thought of this Washington." In the book *Young Washington*, Peter Stark wrote, "Washington was accused of being a war criminal, an assassin, an incompetent leader, negligent, and an international embarrassment. The war that he touched off would last seven years and spread around the world."

The French could have taken Washington prisoner, but they were anxious to avoid a war that could strip them of their fur trading territories and promising settlements in New France. The mood in Britain was very different. War hawks, such as the Duke of Halifax and William Pitt, Pittsburgh's namesake, wanted to renew hostilities with France and saw Washington's defeat as a ripe excuse. The British countered with what they thought would be a knockout punch. They organized an army headed by Braddock to rout the French from their forts.

King George II promoted Braddock, a respected veteran, to major general and made him military commander of all British military forces in North America. On November 14, 1754, Parliament approved one million pounds (roughly $200 million in 2021) for the military effort.[9] The colonies were expected to kick in money, troops, wagons, drivers, and supplies to boost his command of the Forty-Fourth and Forty-Eighth Regiments of Foot, about 1,350 men brought from Ireland. Drafts were conducted to fill out the muster rolls. "So odious was their destined service, however, that every effort of the officers could not restrain desertion. Many of the new drafts or enlistments, too, consisted of the worst class of men, who, had they not been in the army, would probably have been in Bridewell; and this did not tend to elevate the personal standard of the two regiments," wrote Winthrop Sargent in his 1854 classic published by the Historical Society of Pennsylvania, *The History of an Expedition Against Fort DuQuesne, in 1755: Under Major-General Edward Braddock*.[10] "Under convoy of two men-of-war, thirteen transports and three ordnance store-ships had left the Cove of Cork on the 14th of January, 1755; having on the last day taken on board £14,000 in specie."

Braddock arrived in America on February 20, 1755, and created a stir. The governors of Maryland and Virginia said they would provide the 150 wagons needed to carry the baggage. British colonial troops arrived from New York and South Carolina, and colonial militia arrived from Virginia and North Carolina. Some of the colonial governments took umbrage at his demands. The assembly in Pennsylvania denied the request for money and troops. There was some concern that financial interests of the Ohio Company were a motivation for the military expedition. Dinwiddie's investment in the company was a problem for some colonial legislators.

Washington wanted to join the expedition, and Braddock, aware of Washington's regional knowledge, welcomed his involvement but could not give him an officer's rank. The king had ordered

---

[9] Winthrop Sargent, *The History of an Expedition against Fort DuQuesne, in 1755: Under Major-General Edward Braddock*, 133, https://ia800208.us.archive.org/29/items/historyofexpedit00sarg/historyofexpedit00sarg.pdfhttps://ia800208.us.archive.org/29/items/historyofexpedit00sarg/historyofexpedit00sarg.pdf.

[10] Ibid., 135.

the previous November that no colonial officer could outrank any British officer. Washington was not happy; he would be subservient to every British officer. So he joined as a volunteer on Braddock's personal staff. He was officially an aide-de-camp.

Benjamin Franklin, the postmaster general of Pennsylvania, then became involved to assuage any ill feelings Braddock might hold. He explained the situation in his autobiography: "Our Assembly, apprehending from some Information, that he had conceived violent prejudices against them…wish'd me to wait upon him, not as from them, but as Postmaster Gen." He met Braddock in Frederick, Maryland, where the general was "impatiently" waiting for the return of agents who were sent to collect baggage wagons that had been promised by Maryland and Virginia. "I stayed with him several days, Din'd with him daily, and had full Opportunity of removing from all his Prejudices." Braddock was angry, however, that only twenty-five wagons had been provided and some of those were unusable.

Franklin then made the extraordinary offer to supply the wagons from Pennsylvania. After agreeing to terms, Franklin proceeded to southeastern Pennsylvania, where he promised that farmers would be paid in aggregate "upwards of 30,000 pounds in Silver and Gold in the King's Money." He told them horses, wagons, and drivers would be needed for about 120 days and then returned. "The service will be light and easy," he assured them in a printed handbill.[11] The alternative, he said, could be the conscription of the wagons because Braddock and his officers were in a bad temper. Braddock provided Franklin an eight-hundred-pound advance, and Franklin added another two hundred pounds of his own money.

"In two weeks, the 150 Waggons with 259 carrying Horses were on their March for the camp," Franklin reported. The owners insisted on Franklin's bond in case any horses or wagons didn't return. He agreed in what turned out to be a very bad bet on his part.

Referring to Franklin's role, Braddock said that Maryland and Virginia had promised everything and performed nothing and the

---

[11] National Archives Founders Online. "Advertisement for Wagons, 26 April 1755," https://founders.archives.gov/documents/Franklin/01-06-02-0009.

Pennsylvanians had promised nothing and had performed everything.[12] Virginian teamsters, such as Daniel Morgan and Daniel Boone, were hired at exorbitant rates.

Franklin also gave Braddock some excellent advice. He said the general should guard against an ambush by Native warriors on his stretched-out four-mile line as it moved through the wilderness. "He smil'd at my Ignorance, and repl'd, 'These savages may indeed be a formidable Enemy to your raw American Militia; but upon the King's Regular and disciplin'd Troops, Sir, it is impossible that they should make any Impression.'"

Braddock's army left its base at Fort Cumberland, Maryland, on May 29, 1755. Fort Duquesne was 110 miles away across the heavily forested Allegheny Mountains. The second obstacle was getting the army, artillery, and baggage train over the mountains following an old trail that had been improved by the Ohio Company and was called Nemacolin's Path. The frontiersman Gist, who had guided Washington to Fort Le Boeuf, played an important role in the road improvement project.

The tortuous work of converting the path to a wagon trace for Braddock's army began with a detachment led by Lieutenant Colonel John St. Clair. His group included two engineers, a British naval officer, six seamen, and a few Native Americans. One hundred soldiers worked on the road in one-hundred-yard sections at a time. They were protected by another one hundred. Braddock added three hundred more soldiers so the road could be made passable for wagons carrying siege guns to be used at Fort Duquesne. The slow work involved cutting old-growth timber, removing boulders, leveling the ground, and making swamps passable, up and down mountains and through valleys.

---

[12] National Archives Founders Online, "To Benjamin Franklin from Edward Braddock, 29 May 1755," https://founders.archives.gov/documents/Franklin/01-06-02-0034National.

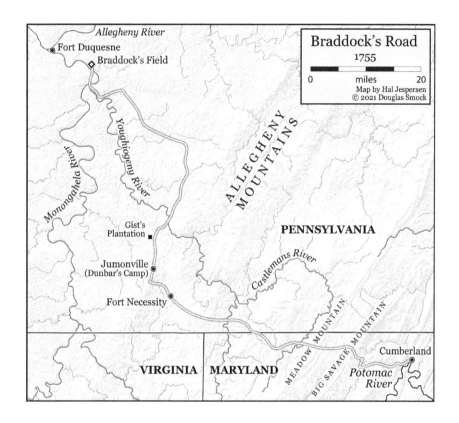

The construction of a military road to accommodate supply wagons and siege cannons through the Allegheny Mountains was a significant undertaking. Braddock's engineers followed a trail that had been improved by a land speculation company based in Virginia. A group called the Braddock Road Preservation Association holds a well-attended annual conference at Jumonville.

A group called the Braddock Road Preservation Association (BRPA) was founded In 1988 to mark and preserve traces of the road. The group conducts a seminar annually in November to discuss Braddock and related topics. Artifacts collected by the group are housed in a small museum in buildings built at Jumonville for orphans of Civil War veterans. The location is near the sites of Braddock's supply depot and the ambush that started the war.

Braddock Road "is one of the best-known icons of American history," wrote Norman L. Baker, historian of the French and Indian War Foundation and active participant in the BRPA. The road was a great feat of colonial engineering, but a painfully slow one for an army in a hurry. To speed the trip, Braddock divided his forces into a flying column of 1,300 to 1,400, followed by a supply force of 700 to 800 headed by Colonel Thomas Dunbar. On the way to Fort Duquesne, they walked past the remains of Fort Necessity and the 40 soldiers who died in the brief battle. They feared an ambush in the Great Meadows, but they passed without incident.

Also headed toward Fort Duquesne from the opposite direction were hundreds of Native Americans allied to the French.

An estimated 650 Natives participated in the battle. They came from twenty different tribal nations from the St. Lawrence Valley, the Ohio territory, and as far west as present-day Wisconsin. Historian Paul E. Kooperman estimated that more than 90 percent might have come from areas around the Great Lakes. "On the whole, the local tribes were straddling the fence, waiting to see which way the nascent war would turn," he wrote in *Braddock at the Monongahela*. There would have been no victory without the Natives, not even close. Their numbers were important, but so was their stealthy fighting style, their ability to frighten British regulars with their fearsome cries, and also their intense, if disorganized, approach to the battle.

Why did they come from so far away? Why were they so committed to the battle? Why were the French so much better than the English at enlisting Native support?

Commercial interests were important. The Natives felt the French would protect their income from the fur trade, while English settlers were a threat. The French had joined forces with Native allies (Ottawa, Miami, and Sioux) to fight the Fox tribe over fur trading rights from 1712 to 1733 in present-day Michigan and Wisconsin. The English and Dutch had supported the Iroquois in an earlier battle for hunting rights in the frontier. The Iroquois succeeded and were nominally fighting partners of the English.

One French fur trader possibly played a role in whipping up Native support and leading them to the battle scene. He was Charles Michel Mouet de Langlade, who lived in present-day Green Bay, Wisconsin. His mother was the daughter of an Ottawa chief, and his father was a French fur trader and French officer. Langlade was born at Fort Michilimackinac, located in the strait of land separating Lakes Huron and Superior. The father of the French commanding officer in the Battle of the Monongahela, Captain Daniel Lienard de Beaujeu, had been commandant of the fort.

Langlade was also a low-ranking French officer but did not participate in the French side of the Battle of the Monongahela. He claimed he led and fought with his fellow Ottawa tribe at the battle, but many historians are skeptical because there is no mention of him in records or personal accounts of the battle. A painting commissioned by the Wisconsin Historical Society showed Langlade directing a Native assault on Braddock's troops. He was sometimes called the Father of Wisconsin. There's no question that Langlade had been active in supporting the French. For example, in 1752, he had been a leader of French and Native forces that destroyed a British fur trading post in present-day Ohio.

The French, in general, worked harder to win favor with the Natives. Braddock was personally disdainful of Native support, while Beaujeu embraced it.

The garrison at Fort Duquesne had 258 men in the winter of 1754–1755, with another 100 Native allies. About 460 more were available at other outposts in the region, according to Professor David Preston in the book *Braddock's Defeat*. The fort was undersized, subject to massive springtime floods, and incapable of withstanding a siege, particularly close-in pounding by British cannon. Winthrop Sargent estimated the garrison at Fort Duquesne in April at "scarce 200," including French and Native allies, who lived in forty bark cabins outside the fort.[13]

Reinforcement from French Canada, preferably with new leadership, was essential to defeat the British Army. A surprise French

---

[13] Sargent, *History of an Expedition*, 187.

attack on a force en route was the preferred defense. River crossings were particularly ideal locations for an attack.

To head up the French reinforcements, Duquesne appointed Captain Beaujeu, who was born in New France and was a veteran of the Battle of Grand Pré, which slowed a British advance in present-day Nova Scotia. One of his gifts was his ability to work well with Native tribes, and he often wore a headdress and other Native gear. The action at Grand Pré included Native allies.

Beaujeu's route from Montreal to Fort Duquesne was much longer than Braddock's, but there were no mountains to climb. There was a well-developed French water route almost the entire way.

Captain Beaujeu, previously in charge of Fort Niagara, had a gift for logistics: he organized a roughly seven-hundred-man, forty-boat expedition for the 670-mile trip down the St. Lawrence River to Lake Ontario to Lake Erie, and then south at present-day Erie, Pennsylvania, via Frensch Creek and the Allegheny River. Two significant portages were required, around Niagara Falls and from Lake Erie to the French Creek, which in June was (and is today) quite shallow and littered with fallen trees and large rocks. Beaujeu's expedition included horses for the portages. The Niagara Falls portage began about six miles below the falls at a Seneca village and climbed to a point about two miles above the falls.

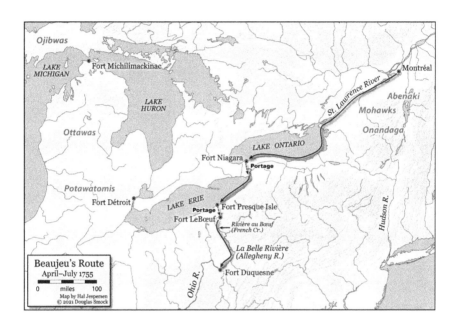

The French moved to Fort Duquesne mostly through water routes but had to make two difficult portages, including around Niagara Falls. The Native tribes came from the St. Lawrence River and Great Lakes areas. Fort Duquesne was located at the "Forks of the Ohio," present-day Pittsburgh. It was the gateway to French New Orleans.

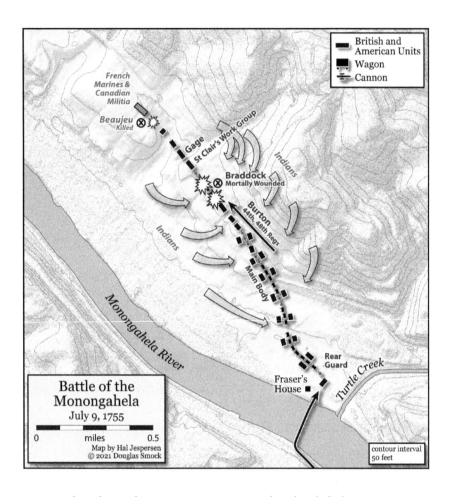

French and British troops ran into one another shortly before 1:00 p.m. after Braddock's troops had crossed the Monongahela River and were ascending a slope in present-day North Braddock, Pennsylvania. Chaos reigned as Native warriors attacked both flanks of British and colonial soldiers. Advancing troops commanded by Lieutenant Colonel Ralph Burton collided with Lieutenant Colonel Thomas Gage's retreating troops on a just-built twelve-foot-wide dirt road. The battle was over by four thirty. About three out of four of Braddock's troops were dead or wounded. The site of Braddock's wounding is the author's estimate based on battle reports.

Part of the route had been developed by the French for fur trading. Especially designed canoes paddled by nine to twelve people regularly carried goods from Montreal to depots at the west end of Lake Superior. Called canots du maître, they hugged the shore to avoid storms. Shallow-draft boats had to be built to navigate the creek that began near Fort LeBoeuf.[14] One of those boats made next to the fort is on display in the Fort LeBoeuf Museum. The troops garrisoned at Fort LeBoeuf two years earlier had been ordered to make the creek navigable. A reproduction of a canot du maître made in 2013 by master canoe builder Richard M. Nash, of Dorset, Ontario, is on display at the Canadian Museum of History in Gatineau, Quebec.[15] The portage road starting at Fort de la Presqu'île was about nineteen miles long, and most of it is now called the Old French Road.

Beaujeu's group left Montreal April 23, 1755, and arrived at Fort Duquesne at the end of June. Along the way, Beaujeu received urgent messages from Claude-Pierre Pécaudy de Contrecoeur, the overwhelmed commander at Fort Duquesne: hurry up. Credible information had been received that British regular troops reinforced with colonial militia were en route to Fort Duquesne with a dozen cannon. Both Beaujeu and Braddock had intelligence of each other's movements and knew it was a life-and-death race.

After his combatants were assembled, Beaujeu made the obvious decision to attack Braddock in the wilderness outside the fort. First, he had to convince Contrecoeur, and then the Native Americans, who particularly feared the English cannon. He reportedly said, "I am determined to go ahead and meet the enemy. What! Will you let your father go by himself? I am sure to beat them."

At 8:00 a.m. on July 9, 1755, he led a force of 254 French Canadians and six hundred to seven hundred Natives against Braddock's advance detached group (or flying column), which included British regulars and

---

[14] Jim Edwards, museum coordinator at Fort LeBoeuf Historical Society, Waterford, Pennsylvania, discussion with author, June 8, 2019.
[15] Tim Foran, "Toward the Confluence: The Canot du Maître in the Canadian History Hall," Musée Canadien de l'Histoire, https://www.historymuseum.ca/blog/a-meeting-point-the-canot-du-maitre-in-the-canadian-history-hall/.

colonial militia. He led his force northeast out of the fort on a wooded path, then turned east and then south toward the Monongahela River, following established trails that have been identified by Professor David Preston. It was about twelve miles away by trail.

Beaujeu had hoped to catch Braddock's army while it was crossing the Monongahela River but instead ran right into an elite unit of grenadiers at the head of a long column on a slightly rising hill about 1.2 miles from the river. The area around the path was mostly wooded. To the right of Braddock's line, the hill rose. To the left, there was a steady drop back to the river. The two sides ran into each other close to 1:00 p.m.

The Natives were armed with smoothbore muskets (as were the French and British forces), tomahawks, knives, and clubs. Like Braddock's army, the French force was a combination of regulars and militias.

Native scouts had been closely watching the advance of Braddock's army for some time. There were signs of Natives in the area, and British lieutenant colonel Thomas Gage was on alert when he crossed the shallow, two-hundred-yard-wide Monongahela with two six-pounder cannons. Two river crossings the morning of July 9 were not contested. Engineers had time to carve out a road up six- to twelve-foot-high muddy riverbanks.

Battle of the Monongahela
Order of Battle

British Army
1,300 to 1,400
Major General Edward Braddock, commanding
George Washington, aide-de-camp
Brevet Captain Robert Orme, aide-de-camp
44th Regiment of Foot: Colonel Peter Halkett
48th Regiment of Foot: Lieutenant Colonel Ralph Burton

3rd Independent New York Company: Captain John Rutherford
4th Independent New York Company: Captain Horatio Gates
3rd Independent South Carolina Company: Captain Paul Demere
Royal Artillery (six 12-pounders, six 6-pounders, 4 howitzers, and around 30 cohorn mortars): Captain Thomas Orde
Royal Navy, 33 sailors
Native scouts, 7
Provincial troops
Virginia militia
North Carolina militia

French Forces
About 900
Captain Daniel Liénard de Beaujeu, commanding (killed in combat)
Captain Jean Daniel Dumas, replaced Beaujeau
Compagnies Franches de la Marine, 108
Canadian militia, 146
Native Americans (Seven Nations of Canada, Ottawa, Ojibwa, Potawatomi, and others), 600 to 700

Members of two grenadier companies, a total of about 150 to 200, were in front as the British moved away from the river and toward Fort Duquesne. Another 110 men walked the flanks outside the column, out about one hundred or so yards on each side. The main body of the Army with Braddock and Washington was trailing by about six-tenths of a mile, following a road construction crew. There was no meaningful forward reconnaissance, one of the first of the serious mistakes made by Braddock. Military historians also fault Braddock for not moving the advance column farther ahead of the main body.

The main troops were moving through a section of Fraser's farm, and some of the area had been cleared. The advance troops moved into a forest, following the edge of a ridgeline about 110 feet above the Monongahela River. On their right, the ridge rose another 320 feet higher. British scouts raced back with reports of the advancing French column.

First-person accounts from both sides about what happened next were confusing, conflicting, and often self-serving. Some soldiers who claimed to be at the battle made such egregious errors in their accounts that some historians questioned their honesty. It is clear that chaos and confusion ensued very soon after the battle started. Most accounts agreed that the French and English columns met head-on and were surprised to see each other. There was no ambush.

The beginning of the battle was a debacle for the French. In the words of French captain Jean Daniel Dumas, "Beaujeu attacked the enemy with much daring, but with his troops in total disorder. We fired our first volley while they were out of range. The enemy waited until they were nearer before firing. And in the first moment of combat, one hundred militiamen—one-half of our forces—shamelessly turned tail."

Following is the view from Braddock's position as recorded in the journal of one of his aides, Brevet Captain Robert Orme: "No sooner were the pickets upon their respective flanks, and the word given to march, but we heard an excessive quick and heavy firing in the front. The General imagining the advanced parties were very warmly attacked, and being willing to free himself from the incumbrance of the baggage, order'd Lt. Col. Burton to reinforce them with the vanguard, and the line to halt. According to this disposition, eight hundred men were detached from the line, free from all embarrassments, and four hundred were left for the defence of the Artillery and baggage, posted in such a manner as to secure them from any attack or insults."[16]

At the front of the line, Beaujeu ordered the remaining militiamen and Native warriors to attack along both flanks, and then he fell

---

[16] Sargent, *History of an Expedition*, 354.

mortally wounded. Command passed to Dumas, whose subsequent battle report embellished his leadership. The British were immediately flummoxed as Native warriors ran from tree to tree and poured fire along the column. They were described as almost invisible. Only very small numbers were seen at one time. Some fired from a ravine at the base of a hill on the right flank. Flankers were the first to fall. Some raced back to the main column, creating terror.

The beginning of the battle was described by the young personal servant to Captain Robert Cholmley, who was located about one hundred yards behind the grenadiers: "Immediately [the warriors] began to engage us in a half moon and still continued surrounding us more and more… My master died before we were 10 minutes engaged. They continually made us retreat… We were drawn up in large bodies together, a ready mark."

Efforts by Gage to reinforce flankers on the right failed. Fire from the ridgeline into the main column became devastating. Native warriors displayed scalps on trees, further striking terror into the British. One British soldier wrote this account: "The men from what stories that had heard of the Indians, in regard to their scalping, and mohawking [tomahawking] were so panic struck, that their officers had little or no command over them."

Efforts by Burton to form a line facing the ridge were disrupted by Gage's retreating men in a twelve-foot-wide road, according to Orme's journal. "The whole were now got together in great confusion. The colours were advanced in different places, to separate the men of the two regiments. The General ordered the officers to endeavour to form the men, and to tell them off into small divisions and to advance with them; but neither entreaties nor threats could prevail. The advanced flank parties, which were left for the security of the baggage, all but one ran in."[17]

British fire became disorganized, and some flankers were killed by friendly fire, now usually replaced by the term *fratricide*. Only about twenty-five of the original grenadiers survived the fight. About a half mile back, Braddock, with Washington in his command party, tried to deploy the main force in a defensive posture, with three

---

[17] Ibid., 355.

twelve-pound cannons defending the left flank.[18] Braddock and Washington also moved forward. As Braddock advanced, he charged any soldiers hiding behind trees, calling them cowards and even striking them with the flat side of his sword.

A British officer wrote in a letter later that month, "The yell of the Indians is fresh in my ear, and the terrific sound will haunt me until the hour of my dissolution. I cannot describe the horrors of that scene."

Late in the battle, Washington said he appealed to Braddock to allow him to "head the Provincials and engage the enemy in their own way." Braddock refused. An earlier effort by Captain Edmond Waggoner (spelled differently in various accounts) and Virginia rangers to take the ridge had met with a barrage of fire from British soldiers. Fifty of the militiamen were victims of fratricide after they had reached the brow of the hill and cleared warriors from behind a large log. A London newspaper's account of the battle, published in October 1755, quoted an anonymous British officer: "Capt. Waggoner, with 170 Virginians, went up where the enemy was hid and routed them: But O unhappy! our infatuateds seeing a smoke, fired, and killed him with several of his men." In David Preston's opinion, the British could still have won if Braddock had allowed Washington to charge the hill.[19]

Warrior marksmen targeted mounted British officers, most of whom were quickly removed from the fight. Two horses were shot from under Washington. When Braddock mounted a fifth horse, he was shot in the chest. Braddock asked that his body be left on the field, but it was moved to the back.

Orme described the end of the battle: "When the men had fired away all their ammunition and the General and most of the officers were wounded, they by one common consent left the field, running off with the greatest precipitation. About fifty Indians pursued us to the river, and killed several men in the passage. The officers used all possible endeavours to stop the men, and to prevail upon them to

---

[18] Ibid., 356.
[19] Presentation by Professor David Preston at the Braddock Road Preservation Society's annual French and Indian War seminar at Jumonville in Hopwood, Pennsylvania, November 4, 2015.

rally, but a great number of them threw away their arms and ammunition, and even their clothes, to escape the faster."[20]

Twenty-year-old Daniel Boone, a teamster, joined others in removing harnesses from wagon horses and riding them back across the Monongahela. After Braddock's wounding, a general retreat was ordered. The Native warriors launched a deadly assault as the British attempted to pull back while maintaining fire. It was a panicky retreat, remembered this way by Washington: "Despite every effort to the contrary, [the British] broke and ran as sheep before the hound." The charge by the remaining French and Natives was restrained by a rear guard of 110 Americans: the South Carolina Independent Company and the First Virginia Ranger Company. They were experienced frontier fighters and were positioned behind trees on the banks of the Monongahela.

An artist named Paul Weber imagined what the battlefield looked like in early 1755. The view shows the field from the opposite side of the Monongahela River. Indians enveloped Braddock's column and fired as they ran from

---

[20] Paul Kopperman, *Battle at the Monongahela*, 215.

tree to tree. The battle began 1.2 miles from the river. The Edgar Thomson Steel Works now covers the area near the river. (Wikimedia Commons)

The battle had lasted more than three hours. Total French and Native casualties were estimated at just around 50. There were 456 British and American dead, and about as many more wounded. Of the 583 who escaped safely, only 25 were commissioned officers.[21] Many of those captured were later killed by Native warriors at Fort Duquesne. The chaos contributed to significant fratricide. Incredibly, in Washington's opinion, fratricide may have represented two-thirds of the British casualties.

Every battle has myths and legends, and a persistent story was that Braddock was killed by one of his own men. Tom Fawcett, a Pennsylvanian supplementing the Forty-Eighth Regiment of Foot, actually claimed to have fired the fatal shot. The issue is dissected in Paul E. Kooperman's book *Braddock at the Monongahela*.

The scalped and mutilated bodies on the field were left to rot for three years. After Forbes captured Fort Duquesne in 1758, he sent a burial party to Braddock's Field. Major Peter Halkett, of Forbes's staff, went to the site with a warrior who had been in the battle in an effort to find the remains of his father and brother, Peter Halkett, commander of the Forty-Fourth Regiment of Foot, and James Halkett, a major in the regiment, respectively. Their remains were found under a tree, in an embrace. They were buried and covered with a Highland plaid. Streets were later named in their honor in Pittsburgh, Braddock, and nearby McKeesport.

Most of the remains were buried in a trench that has never been located. According to local legend, a crew laying a new line for the Pennsylvania Railroad dug up skeletons and reinterred them.[22] There are no records to support the claim, however. Braddock died and was buried on the chaotic retreat ironically very close to the Great Meadows. Some of his last words were, "Who would have thought it?" He gave Washington a broad red sash he had worn as a sign of

---

[21] Sargent, *History of an Expedition*, 238.
[22] Robert T. Messner, *Reflections from Braddock's Battlefield* (2005), 94.

command. The sash is one of the prized possessions of the curators at Mount Vernon, Washington's home in Virginia.[23]

Many of the horses and wagons delivered through Franklin's efforts were lost in the battle and its aftermath. Franklin's debts amounted to twenty thousand pounds, and angry Pennsylvania farmers sued him. He appealed for relief to Governor William Shirley of Massachusetts, who had assumed North American military command after Braddock's death. Governor Shirley appointed a commission to investigate the claims and followed up with payment. Shirley's son William was killed in the Battle of the Monongahela while acting as Braddock's secretary. In Philadelphia, Franklin was disgusted that the retreating British Army refused to release indentured servants the farmers had provided to drive the wagons.

Braddock took much of the criticism for his army's failure. But one of his staff members and confidants, Robert Orme, tried to shift the blame to Gage for failing to restrain his fleeing troops. Gage stated his defense in a public declaration in Franklin's *Pennsylvania Gazette* on September 4. In the opinion of Professor John Richard Alden, writing in *General Gage in America*, Orme's "charge was apparently without substantial basis of fact." Gage was denied a promotion to replace Halkett as colonel of the Forty-Fourth Regiment, but he became commander in chief of the British Army in North America in 1763. Washington and Gage exchanged letters and were friendly after the battle, but they would soon become enemies. They led opposing armies during the Siege of Boston in 1775 to 1776.

Other Braddock campaign veterans also became important players in the Revolutionary War. Lieutenant Charles Lee of Halkett's Forty-Fourth switched sides and was Washington's second-in-command during the Siege of Boston. Captain Horatio Gates also became a commander in the Continental Army. Daniel Morgan, a twenty-year-old teamster who probably was in Dunbar's rear group, became a general in Washington's

---

[23] "Braddock Sash," Mount Vernon Ladies' Association, https://emuseum.mountvernon.org/objects/296/braddock-sash;jsessionid=C5B01BF6FA66D4D8EDFA01D2F08E2997?ctx=a394eb86cf9e3f35ab4f6f7559f87cf1aaceac3a&idx=17.

army, whose performance at the Battle of Cowpens is still studied today. Lee probably also was at Dunbar's camp during the battle.

The field where Braddock was mortally wounded became a well-known gathering place. Some seven thousand southwestern Pennsylvania farmers rallied there on August 1, 1794, to protest a federal tax on whiskey sales during a minirevolt called the Whiskey Rebellion. It was an important early test for President George Washington.

More than one hundred years after the battle, an amateur historian named William Coleman visited Braddock's Field. He was also an agent for Andrew Carnegie and convinced the entrepreneur that the area would be a perfect site for a showcase steel mill he was planning to build with the groundbreaking Bessemer iron reduction process. Today the mill occupies the area where Braddock's army crossed the Monongahela and where rear guards protected survivors as they recrossed the river.

Local officials commissioned a statue of George Washington in 1930, and it remains the only monument on the field. The state historical marker at the left was originally misplaced in an adjacent town. (Wikimedia Commons)

Walking the field today requires a lot of imagination. When I walk from the point of first contact down toward the Monongahela River, I have no sense an important battle took place here, with the exception of a state historical marker at the Washington statue and a hard-to-find placard embedded in the wall of an apartment building that indicates a point of Braddock's advance. A golf course with a beautiful view was built on top of the hill used by Native warriors. There are plenty of empty lots, dilapidated buildings, and industrial businesses close to the river. Population in the area dropped from twenty thousand to two thousand in the last hundred years. The prize jewel in the neighborhood is an imposing stone-and-brick library that Carnegie established near his first steel mill. It was the first in what became a global network of 2,500 free public libraries.[24] Carnegie, who personally dedicated the library in 1889, included a swimming pool and a bathhouse where millworkers could shower. Fundraising for a major renovation of the library was announced in 2019.

Today a privately funded museum is located on the battlefield. The field is not a local, state, or national military site, while Fort Necessity is a national military park with a reconstructed fort. The museum would not exist if not for the efforts of Robert Messner, a soft-spoken retired attorney who lives five miles north of the battlefield.

"In the summer of 1984 after reading about George Washington's participation in Braddock's Defeat, I traveled to the riverfront in Braddock, Pennsylvania," wrote Messner in *Reflections from Braddock's Battlefield*.[25] "Encountering a fisherman there, I enquired whether he had any idea where it was that the Braddock Expedition had waded across the (now deep) Monongahela River." He had no idea but suggested Messner inquire at the nearby Carnegie Library. "There are some weird people up there who worry about that kind of thing," he said.

Determined to become one of those weird people, Messner joined a local historical society, researched and wrote more than fifty

---

[24] Braddock Carnegie Library Association, "The First 130 Years," http://braddockcarnegielibrary.org/our-histories.

[25] Robert T. Messner, *Reflections from Braddock's Battlefield* (2005).

articles for the group's newsletter, personally acquired many artifacts and paintings, secured some grants, and opened the stand-alone museum in 2012.

To Messner, the battle witnessed the enormous growth of Washington as a leader: "Washington was the only British or colonial leader whose reputation was enhanced by the battle. He was brave under fire, suggesting orders to Braddock that could have ended the slaughter. He had developed significantly since his experiences at Jumonville Glen and Fort Necessity. His conduct became legendary, and his reputation was widely advanced by surviving colonial soldiers. Twenty years later he was named Commanding Officer of colonial troops at the beginning of the American Revolution."[26]

Founding Father and future president John Adams nominated Washington to serve as commander in chief of America's first Army, although other candidates had more military experience, albeit in the British Army. Adams wrote in his diary, "I had no hesitation to declare that I had but one gentleman in my mind for that important command and that was a gentleman from Virginia, who was among us and very well known to all of us; a gentleman, whose skill and experience as an officer, whose indepesndent fortune, great talents and excellent universal character would command the approbation of all America, and unite the cordial exertions of all the colonies better than any other person in the Union."

The growth in Washington was the single most important outcome of the battle. The second was the realization by Washington, Franklin, and many others that the British were beatable. Messner also pointed out that many participants in the campaign, besides Washington, constituted a who's who of American colonial history. The battle was also one of the most significant military victories for Native Americans. The largest defeat of the American military by Native Americans based on casualty count was the Battle of the Wabash River in 1791 in western Ohio, near the Indiana border. Braddock's Defeat is a close second.

---

[26] Interview with author, July 7, 2021.

While Washington is still highly revered in our national consciousness, even he hasn't escaped a rethinking.

In 2019, a Depression-era mural in a San Francisco high school depicting key aspects of Washington's life, including the debacle at Jumonville and slaves working at Mount Vernon, became a test case of how America wanted to remember its first president. The mural was denounced by a few historians and Native Americans as glorifying White supremacy and dehumanizing Native Americans. The irony is that the painter was a communist who clearly wanted to point out what he considered truths about Washington's life. The city's school board initially voted to paint over the mural, then shifted course after complaints. The mural is now covered with panels, apparently awaiting the next spin in how we choose to remember our history. No one ever questioned the accuracy of the mural. The controversy demonstrated the difficulties in presenting unpleasant historical truths, particularly in schools. A large mural in a school lobby with outdated depictions of Native Americans and slaves, however, may not have been the best test case.

When I first met with Messner at his museum in 2016, he said he wanted to educate local schoolchildren about the battle as well as provide a tourism boost to the depressed area. Groups of local schoolchildren toured the museum on field trips, and many walked over to the nearby George Washington statue. If Messner was there, they got a heartfelt history lesson.

The carefully curated museum includes many items beyond the typical artifacts. For example, Messner showed me a map on the wall of the battlefield drawn by one of Carnegie's engineers who had been working on plans for the Edgar Thomson (ET) Works. It was the first serious map of the field drawn since crude French versions in 1755 and a finely detailed map made by an engineer on Braddock's staff. Braddock historian David Preston has tweaked those maps and even made some corrections, such as the exact location of the British column. A local Eagle Scout developed a walking tour of key points of the battle.

It's hard to say why the National Park Service built a beautiful military park at Fort Necessity and did nothing at Braddock's Field. Messner had no idea when I discussed the issue with him in 2021.

Maybe the industrial nature of the neighborhood was a factor. The ET Works survived the domestic steel industry collapse of the 1980s, but employment is far below its peak. Neighboring steel plants in Homestead and McKeesport did close, leaving the area distressed. A much-hoped-for renovation of the Braddock plant was canceled in 2021 as US Steel (the successor company to Carnegie) said it needed to prioritize greener investment in its push toward reduced carbon emissions.

In 2018, because of advancing age and declining health, Messner donated the museum to a group that operates Fort Ligonier, a restoration of one of the forts built in the Forbes expedition. The new operators renovated the museum and brought some marketing energy that resulted in an increase in visitors until COVID-19 struck in 2020. Mary Magnes, the new executive director of Braddock's Battlefield History Center, said she hopes annual attendance will reach 1,500 in 2023, up from 1,100 in 2019. Plans include capital improvements and expanded educational outreach, but new funding will be required. "Braddock's Battlefield History Center is a well-kept secret, and we're trying to change that," Magnes told me in a phone interview after the museum reopened in 2021.[27]

A former classroom teacher, Magnes would like to see more attention paid in schools to the French and Indian War and in Washington's role. "In order to understand the Revolutionary War, you first have to understand the French and Indian War and the impact it had on George Washington," she said.

The costs incurred by the British in fighting the French in America resulted in taxes that triggered the American Revolution. The experience gained by Washington in that fighting steeled him to lead the colonies to victory in the American Revolution.

---

[27] Interview with the author, July 2, 2021.

CHAPTER 3

Daniel Morgan and Cowpens

Seldom has a battle, in which greater numbers were not engaged, been so important in its consequences as that of Cowpens.

—John Marshall,
Continental soldier,
Virginia politician, Supreme Court justice

Cowpens may be one of the most important battles ever fought on American soil from the standpoint of the tactical lessons one can learn from it.

—Lieutenant Colonel John Moncure,
US Army Combat Studies Institute

The eight-year-long Revolutionary War pivoted on the South Carolina grazing fields of Cowpens, where a veteran American commander faced off against a brash, talented English cavalry officer. Their personalities—both troubled—and the significance of the American victory make Cowpens particularly interesting. It is a stunning example of the role of local militia. The theme of remembrance also resonates. Who was glorified? Who was vilified? Who was forgotten? Why?

The war in the North had come to a standstill in 1778. The British had firm control of New York City, but the Continentals had a strong defensive position on the Hudson River at West Point and also held

New Jersey. The British were able to occupy coastal Northern cities at will, while George Washington's Continental Army was victorious only in indirect actions, such as Trenton and Monmouth. His army had improved after training by Friedrich von Steuben at Valley Forge but was still no match for the British regulars reinforced with German troops.

In 1777, the British suffered a significant defeat at Saratoga, New York, a turning point that brought in support from European powers, notably France. British commander in chief Henry Clinton felt his best shot at victory was in the Southern colonies, where there was space to maneuver and Loyalists could be tapped for combat service. Savannah, Georgia, was already under British control, and Charleston, South Carolina, was an obvious target. Although the French fleet had the potential to harass the sea-lanes, it had not yet become a serious factor in the war.

In May 1780, the British besieged and captured Charleston and its garrison of five thousand headed by General Benjamin Lincoln. It was a major defeat for the new American republic. All the Continental Army in the Carolinas and Georgia was captured. "This might have been the greatest blow to the American cause in the war," wrote John Moncure in an analysis for the US Army Combat Studies Institute.

Using Charleston as an operations base, Clinton dispatched Lieutenant Colonel Banastre Tarleton to chase down colonial militia. One of his victories was at Waxhaws, South Carolina, where his troops were accused of killing soldiers who had surrendered. Patriot soldiers termed the slaughter "Tarleton's quarter," or no mercy.

Clinton returned to New York and appointed Charles Cornwallis as his commander in the South. His assignment was to secure South Carolina first and then North Carolina. In response, Congress dispatched Major General Horatio Gates to the South, but he was routed at Camden, South Carolina, in August when militia forces collapsed. Cornwallis began a move toward Charlotte, North Carolina, and sent a force of Loyalist militia into western South Carolina. They were defeated at the Battle of Kings Mountain on October 7, 1780, by a militia working with frontier sharpshooters.[28]

---

[28] Robert Dunkerly, email message to author, July 15, 2021.

The battle was a prelude to Cowpens. Lord Cornwallis retreated from Charlotte into South Carolina, and the pause gave the Continentals time to execute an important next step.

In October 1780, Washington appointed Nathanael Greene, his best commander, to take charge in the South, replacing Gates. A native of Rhode Island, Greene was an original brigadier general in Washington's army, and he knew Washington's playbook: harass the numerically superior British regulars and their Loyalist militias and avoid a pitched head-to-head battle.

On his way south, Greene stopped in Philadelphia to appeal for support from members of the Continental Congress. The Virginia delegation, in particular, felt pressure from the success of Cornwallis's army. Greene presented them with Washington's instructions as well as a letter he had written: "Whether this appointment is considered a misfortune or otherwise, will depend upon future events. He [Greene] is conscious of his deficiencies, but if he is clothed with proper powers and receives the necessary support, he is not altogether without hopes of prescribing some bounds to the ravages of the enemy… Money is the sinews of war, and without a military chest, it is next to impossible to employ an army to effect."[29]

Congress was sympathetic to his situation, confirming his appointment as commander in the South and adding von Steuben to his command. The Continental Congress passed a resolution directing Southern states to provide soldiers, supplies, and weapons. "So the first step had been taken, and with a promptness and tenacious attitude not exhibited by Congress in some time, Greene was well on his way," wrote Lee P. Anderson in *Forgotten Patriot: The Life and Times of Major-General Nathanael Greene*.

Greene had a start, but he felt his newly formed army was "rather a shadow than a substance." On this thin thread—and on the willingness of the Southern states to rally—hung the future of the country.

He wrote to Washington, "My first objective will be to equip a flying camp to consist of 800 horse (cavalry) and one thousand

---

[29] George Greene, ed., *The Life of Nathanael Greene* (Carlisle, Massachusetts: Applewood Books, 2009), 36.

infantry. This force, with the occasional aid of the militia, will serve to confine the enemy in their limits and render it difficult for them to subsist in the interior country. I see but little prospect of getting a force to contend with the enemy upon equal ground."

Greene appealed to Chief of Artillery Henry Knox for cannons, and he was still woefully short of rifles. He appealed to his friend Joseph Reed, the governor of Pennsylvania, for 4,000, but Reed and the government supply office could only find 1,500. Greene also appealed for clothing and four hundred covered wagons. What was left of Gate's army in Salisbury, North Carolina, lacked basic needs from shoes to coats. Only 800 of 2,307 were described as fully clothed and equipped.

Before he left Philadelphia to take command of his Southern army, Greene wrote Washington a prescient thought: "The British might receive a stunning blow in Virginia if (French naval officers) Count Rochambeau and Admiral Ternay would suddenly embark their troops, and land in Virginia." Washington surely made a note.

On December 1, 1780, Greene took command of the Southern army from Gates. His first orders were to deploy scouts to gather intelligence on the navigability of rivers and the condition of local roads. In his camp was South Carolina governor John Rutledge, whose home in Charleston had been confiscated by the British. Rutledge promised to help raise militia.

The army Greene inherited from Gates included 900 to 1,000 Continentals, or regular army. The others were state militia. Cornwallis, encamped near Camden, had 3,224 troops, and they were better equipped. In addition, they were reinforced with Major General Alexander Leslie's 1,500.

After raising troops and gathering supplies, Greene made the odd strategic decision of dividing his inferior force into two. Lack of provisions forced his hand, and his troops could forage better when split apart. He dispatched a small force under newly promoted Daniel Morgan to move southwest, with the goals of boosting morale in the South Carolina countryside and threatening British outposts. Greene moved his main force to the Southeast. Cornwallis also divided his troops.

Daniel Morgan as painted by Charles Willson Peale in the 1790s. (Public domain.)

Morgan, now a brigadier general, was given 300 regulars, 80 to 90 light dragoons commanded by Lieutenant Colonel William Washington, more than 130 Virginia militiamen, and almost 200 state troops commanded by Edmund Tate, who had a states troops commission from Virginia. Morgan would be joined by more than 500 local militiamen from at least three states. They would be led by Colonel Andrew Pickens, a veteran whose property had been destroyed by Loyalists. The exact number of militiamen is hard to determine because some, possibly many, turned up at the last minute. The regulars were long-serving veterans, while the state troops enlisted for six to eighteen months. Both were considered more dependable than local militiamen, who sometimes were little more than ad hoc partisans who showed up when they felt they were needed. Many from western South Carolina bolstered Morgan's army at the last moment. For that reason, estimates of his troop strength at Cowpens differed widely.

Morgan's hard-nosed background played an important role in motivating and commanding his troops, particularly the late-arriving backwoodsmen. He had served as a twenty-year-old civilian teamster in General Edward Braddock's army that was routed by a smaller force of French and Native Americans in southwestern Pennsylvania in 1755. Lashed 499 times for striking a British officer, Morgan had a reputation as a drinker and a brawler until he got married and settled down. He became a prosperous, slave-owning farmer in Virginia who helped guard the Ohio frontier. In 1775, he organized a rifle company that became part of George Washington's army in Boston and played important roles in the battles of Quebec and Saratoga.

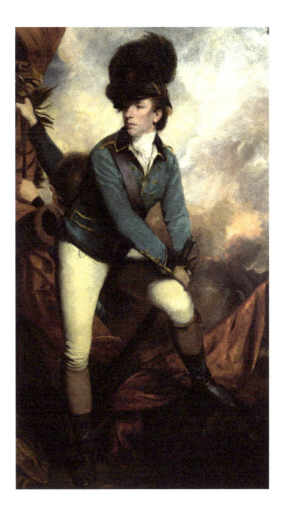

Banastre Tarleton as painted by Joshua Reynolds in 1782. (Public domain.)

The British countered Greene's maneuvers by sending Colonel Banastre Tarleton's British Legion to root Morgan out. Tarleton was already infamous and was often called the Butcher. His British Legion, organized in New York in 1778, wore green uniforms.

Tarleton's force of 1,150 approached Cowpens overnight, hoping to attack Morgan as he was moving. But Morgan had stopped and developed a plan for a battle that is still studied at the US Army

Combat Studies Institute[30] and at West Point.[31] He knew Tarleton was impulsive, very confident, and would attack quickly. Morgan was also concerned his local militia might collapse under fire.

He chose a field for the battle that was in front of a river—almost never a good idea. But Morgan felt the river at their backs might force his militia to hold their ground. Morgan later commented, "As to retreat, it was the very thing I wished to cut off all hope of. I would have thanked Tarleton had he surrounded me with his cavalry. It would have been better than placing my own men in the rear to shoot down those who broke from ranks."[32] Morgan also said he didn't want the militia to have any view of a swamp to which they could escape.[33]

It seems Morgan exaggerated concerns about the militia to make a point. The river was, after all, five miles in the rear. A total envelopment of his troops would have been cataclysmic. Tarleton's mounted raiders would have charged and attacked troops from all sides.

A more important reason for picking the field was its well-known location. Local militia could be told to mobilize quickly at the cattle-roundup area of Cowpens and they knew exactly where to go, in a manner not unlike "minutemen" rushing to Concord, Massachusetts, in 1775. The field also featured a slight rise where Morgan positioned his main line perpendicular to a road. On the con side, the field was lightly wooded, an advantage for Tarleton's cavalry.

Morgan outlined his plan the night before the battle and personally rallied his troops in a frontier version of King Henry V. He moved from campfire to campfire, joking and exhorting men on and telling them to trust "the Old Wagoner." In orders issued to a major who commanded Georgia and South Carolina militia units at Cowpens, Morgan wrote, "As the enemy seems resolved to force us into action, the numbers and spirit of this little band of patriot soldiers seems to justify the General

---

[30] John Moncure, *The Cowpens Staff Ride and Battlefield Tour* (Combat Studies Institute), 43.
[31] Lawrence Babits, communication with author, July 17, 2021.
[32] William Johnson, *Sketches of the Life and Correspondence of Nathanael Greene* (self-published, 1822), 376, Google Books.
[33] Edwin Bearss, *Battle of Cowpens* (Johnson City, Tennessee: The Overmountain Press, 1996), 14.

in the belief that they may be met with confidence and driven back."[34] It was an unintended echo of the words Shakespeare put into King Henry V's mouth before facing a formidable French force at Agincourt in 1415: "We few, we happy few, we band of brothers."

Morgan was a great motivator and a great planner.

Order of the Battle of Cowpens

American Forces
Brigadier General Daniel Morgan
970+
Continental Army: Lieutenant Colonel John Eager Howard
2nd Maryland Regiment, three companies
1st Delaware Regiment, one company
State Militia: Captain Edmund Tate (Virginia)
Local Militia: Colonel Andrew Pickens (Georgia, North Carolina, and South Carolina)
Cavalry
3rd Regiment of Continental Light Dragoons (Virginia), led by Lieutenant Colonel William Washington (80)
Militia cavalry, commanded by James McCall (45 from South Carolina and Georgia)

British Army
Lieutenant Colonel Banastre Tarleton
1,150
British Legion: Dragoons and Infantry
1st Battalion
7th Regiment
71st Regiment
Light Company
Artillery detachment

---

[34] Moncure. "Battle Report of Major Samuel Hammond," 132.

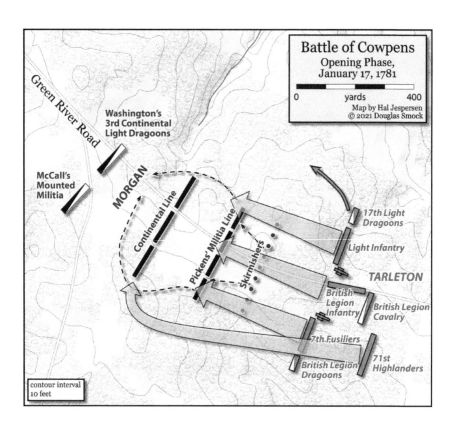

Morgan told the first two lines to shoot and then retreat, pulling the overconfident British into a trap. Recent research indicates that McCall's cavalry was positioned behind the right flank of the Continental Line.

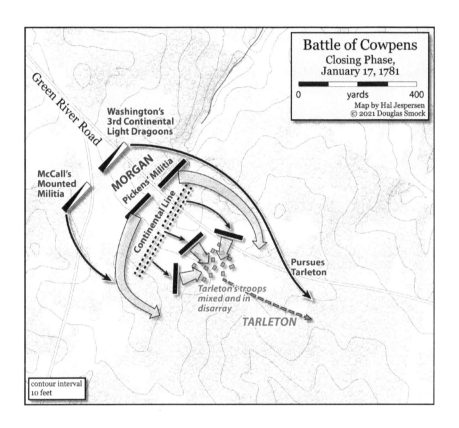

Militia and cavalry enveloped Tarleton's troops after the Continental Line held.

A sign at Cowpens shows the view of the first line of skirmishers across a meadow toward the British line.

This was his battle plan: In the first line were about one hundred riflemen acting as skirmishers. About 150 yards back were the local militia units commanded by Andrew Pickens. Morgan's orders laid out the exact disposition of units along the line. Behind them were the Continental regulars commanded by John Eager Howard.

Morgan told skirmishers, mostly armed with rifles, to shoot British officers and then to fall in with a line of militiamen headed by Pickens. These men were told to fire two or three rounds with their smoothbore muskets then move around and through the flank of the main line to a predesignated rallying area. Each line was progressively stronger. Morgan wanted Tarleton to think the militia was panicking, as they had in previous battles.

Rifles had an effective range of up to three hundred yards but took a minute to load and fire. Muskets could fire three volleys in a minute but with an effective range of just fifty or so yards, according to former National Park Service historian Ed Bearss.

Morgan positioned cavalry on the back side of the rallying area to also block further retreat. The cavalry could then respond to hot spots on the field. Morgan anticipated an overconfident British charge into the main line, with the reformed troops filling in gaps. It was a trap waiting to be sprung. The gambit anticipated the British would be overconfident and charge right into a barrage of fire.

Would Tarleton take the bait?

As Tarleton approached Cowpens after an overnight pursuit, he liked the ground. "The woods were open and free from swamps," he wrote in his report on the battle. He was also under the false impression that there were other British troops in the area. He felt the Americans were vulnerable, and he quickly developed his plan of attack.[35] First he met with his scouts.

"The light infantry were then ordered to the right till they became equal to the flank of the American front line: the legion infantry were added to their left; and under the fire of a three-pounder, this part of the British troops was instructed to advance within three hundred yards of the enemy."

Then "the 7th regiment was commanded to form upon the left of the legion infantry, and the other three-pounder was given to the right division of the 7th. A captain, with fifty dragoons, was placed on each flank of the corps, who formed the British front line."

The First Battalion of the Seventy-First and two hundred cavalrymen were positioned 150 yards in the rear as reserves. "During the execution of these arrangements, the animation of the officers and the alacrity of the soldiers afforded the most promising assurances of success," wrote Tarleton.

After Tarleton ordered an advance at sunrise shortly after 7:30 a.m. on January 17, 1781, his troops received rifle fire from the skirmishers huddled behind trees. After discharging a few rounds,

---

[35] Ibid., 149. Reprinted from Banastre Tarleton's *A History of the Campaigns of 1780 and 1781 in the Southern Provinces of North America* (Dublin: T. Cadill, 1787).

skirmishers fell in with Pickett's militia. That line fired as directed and then retreated (also as directed) around and through the flanks of the third line. As they ran toward the rear, they were chased around Morgan's left flank by British cavalrymen waving sabers. The Continental cavalry, led by Washington, stopped the charge.

The British infantry proceeded forward to the main Continental line, commanded by Howard, who had placed the Maryland and Delaware companies in the middle. Francis Triplett commanded three companies of Virginia militia on the left, while Edmund Tate commanded three companies on the right. The company on the extreme right was led by Captain Andrew Wallace. The soldiers were in line in two ranks.[36]

The British advance stalled under heavy fire. Tarleton ordered his reserves, the Seventy-First Highlanders, into the battle, attacking Howard's right flank. They acted as a reinforcement for David Ogilvie's British Legion Dragoons. An order was issued for Wallace's company to reform so as to be perpendicular to the main line, a maneuver termed *refusing* the line. Most of the company, however, misheard the order and failed to swing after facing and marching to the rear.

Howard explained what happened next in this critical moment: "Morgan, who had been with the militia, quickly rode up to me and expressed apprehensions of the event; but I soon removed his fears by pointing to the line, and observing that the men were not beaten who retreated in that order. He then ordered me to keep with the men, and we came to the rising ground near Washington's horse; and he rode forward to fix on the most proper place for us to halt and face about. In a minute we had a perfect line. The enemy was very near us now. Our men commenced a very destructive fire, which they very little expected, and a few rounds occasioned great disorder in their ranks."[37]

Morgan later called it "a fortunate volley."[38] The lines were less than thirty yards apart.

---

[36] Lawrence Babits, communication with author, July 17, 2021.
[37] Moncure, 127. Reprinted from a letter written by Lieutenant Colonel John E. Howard. Original is owned by the Cowpens National Battlefield, MS 102, box 4.
[38] Ibid., 123.

Tarleton described it this way: "An unexpected fire at this instant from the Americans, who came about as they were retreating, stopped the British, and threw them into confusion. Exertions to make them advance were useless. The part of the cavalry which had not been engaged fell likewise into disorder, and an unaccountable panic extended itself along the whole line. The Americans, who before thought they had lost the action, taking advantage of the present situation, advanced on the British troops and augmented their astonishment."

Robert M. Dunkerly, a National Park Service ranger who has worked at Kings Mountain and studied Cowpens, told me, "The crucial thing here is the mistaken order. The American troops thought it was an order to retreat, not refuse the line, so they marched off in good order. It could have gone downhill fast and spiraled out of control, but Morgan and Howard rescued the situation at just the right moment. Amid the chaos of battle with noise, smoke, confusion, it was a touch-and-go situation, and the fact that the troops were able to reload, turn, fire, and keep their cohesion under those circumstances is an incredible part of the battle."

After the British troops staggered, Howard ordered a bayonet charge, quickly capturing two artillery pieces. Soon they surrendered, including one British officer, who approached Howard for help by pulling on his saddle. "I expressed my displeasure and asked him what he was about," Howard wrote. "The explanation was that they had orders to give no quarter [show no mercy], and they did not expect any." Howard put the officer under guard, and the officer "some years afterwards" sent messages of thanks for saving his life.

After Howard enveloped the left flank of Tarleton's force, what happened next almost simultaneously became a military textbook study. Washington's cavalry swung out behind the left flank of Howard's line and enveloped the other side of Tarleton's troops. Pickens's militia regrouped according to plan and also swept around Howard's line. The British were soon completely surrounded and overwhelmed. Some of Morgan's troops were anxious for revenge, yelling, "Remember Tarleton's quarter!" but Morgan held them back.

In one scene remembered by Major Joseph McJunkin, an officer in Pickens's militia, "some five or six hundred tall, brawny, well-clad soldiers, the flower of the British Army, [were] guarded by a set of militia clad in hunting shirts 'blacked, smoked and greasy.'"[39]

In his report to Greene two days after the battle, Morgan wrote, "It perhaps would be well to remark for the honor of the American arms, that although the progress of this [Tarleton's] corps was marked with burning and devastation, and although they waged the most cruel warfare, not a man was killed, wounded, or even insulted, after he surrendered."

The British had lost 110 killed and 791 captured, including 229 who were wounded. Tarleton left behind two cannons, one hundred horses, and the colors of the Seventh Regiment. Morgan's troops also captured 70 former slaves and returned them to slavery. Morgan kept two of the slaves. There were a dozen Americans killed, with another 69 wounded, according to Morgan, who probably did not include militia casualties.

The battle on the small field was over by 9:00 a.m.

The Continentals pulled out a victory because (1) Morgan had a strong tactical plan built on progressive depth, (2) he had the confidence of his troops, and (3) he held steady and took control when his right flank started to collapse. It was certainly an improbable victory. Morgan was confronted by a better-armed opponent. He was wary of local militia who had collapsed at Camden. The field of open woods favored Tarleton's cavalry.

Chalk one up for the Old Wagoner.

The victory put a nail in the coffin of the British Southern strategy. In the next phase of the campaign, Cornwallis and Greene engaged at Guilford Courthouse in North Carolina. Cornwallis defeated a larger American force, but at a significant cost. His casualties were as much as a quarter of his army.

---

[39] Ibid., 135. Reprinted from *Memoirs of Major Joseph McJunkin: Revolutionary Patriot*, published originally in 1817 in the *Watchman and Observer* of Richmond, Virginia.

Cornwallis decided to move to Virginia, where he could be reinforced with other British troops. Instead, he was trapped at Yorktown, where he surrendered on October 19, 1781. A resolution in the British Parliament to end the war failed by one vote. Lengthy peace negotiations were complicated by America's European allies, and the Treaty of Paris was signed on September 3, 1783. The Continental Army was dissolved except for a frontier outpost at Pittsburgh's Fort Pitt and a caretaker force at West Point.

The peculiar institution of slavery is particularly peculiar when examined through the lens of the Revolutionary War in the South.

In 1775, the besieged royal governor of Virginia, John Murray, Lord Dunmore, declared martial law and offered freedom for slaves owned by patriots if they joined Royal forces. The Virginia legislature saw Dunmore's proclamation as a bid to incite slave riots and responded angrily that it would execute "all negro and other slaves" who left their masters. Slaves were warned that Dunmore's real intent was to sell them in the West Indies.

Dunmore organized three hundred escaped slaves into what he called the Ethiopian Regiment. They wore sashes inscribed with "Liberty to Slaves." Although the men were often used for labor, they saw some combat in two years of service.

In 1779, British commander Henry Clinton freed slaves owned by patriots with no requirement to bear arms. Clinton's edict had more impact than Dumore's proclamation. It's estimated that as many as one hundred thousand slaves escaped into British control, or nearly one in five. Historian Gary Nash called the slave exodus to British lines "the dirty little secret" of the Revolutionary War.

In his *History of the Campaigns of 1780 and 1781*, Banastre Tarleton wrote this about the runaway slaves: "Upon the approach of any detachment of the King's troops, all the negroes, men, women, and children…quitted the plantations and followed the army."

The slavery issue at the battle was explained to me by Lawrence Babits, who wrote one of the best accounts of Cowpens in the book *A Devil of a Whipping: The Battle of Cowpens*. Morgan and his officers took possession of the seventy former slaves traveling with Tarleton as cooks and laborers at the Battle of Cowpens for so-called safekeeping. Babits, who teaches battlefield archaeology at East Carolina University, said, "The idea was that, by giving them to officers on a temporary basis, they would be secure from recapture." Babits added that he was unaware of any of the seventy, including Morgan's two, being returned to their owners.

An 1845 painting of a Cowpens battle scene by William Ranney shows an unnamed Black youth (left) firing his pistol and saving the life of Colonel William Washington (on white horse). (Public domain.)

A well-known 1845 painting of the Battle of Cowpens by William Ranney shows a bugler in Morgan's force shooting a British cavalryman about to strike William Washington with a sword. The bugler is portrayed as a mounted Black youth. Washington had advanced thirty yards in front of his regiment, triggering an attack by three British officers, possibly including Tarleton. An attempt by one officer to strike Washington was stopped by a fast-arriving Continental sergeant. An attempt by a second British officer to kill Washington with a sword blow was stopped by a shot fired from a person described as a boy or waiter. It was assumed by Ranney that the young shooter was Black. There is no record that he was.

Servants and waiters on the British side typically were former patriot-owned slaves. On the Continental side, both races served as servants to the officers. A few African Americans also served as combatants for the Continentals.

The fate of the slaves who joined the British cause was mixed. Many were given certificates of freedom, which became important when the British evacuated New York. Babits told me that the slaves under British Army control were identified with the broad arrow symbol indicative of British property.

When British troops left at the end of the war, their ships departing New York, South Carolina, and Georgia carried several thousand former slaves to freedom in loyalist colonies in Canada, London, and the Caribbean. Those who couldn't fit on the ships were returned to slavery. Of the seven thousand to eight thousand Blacks who left Charleston, South Carolina, "the great majority" were enslaved to departing loyalists, according to Australian historian Cassandra Pybus in her book *Epic Journeys of Freedom: Runaway Slaves of the American Revolution and Their Global Quest for Liberty*. Only about 1,500 who left Charleston were free.

George Washington asked a military contractor named David Parker to try to track down "several" slaves that had escaped from Mount Vernon. Congress had passed a resolution demanding the return of all "negroes and other property." The chief British negotiator, himself an owner of slaves in Florida, agreed to a last-minute handwritten addition to the peace treaty barring the British from "carrying away any negroes or other property," according to Pybus.

The British commander who had already begun evacuations from New York told an upset Washington that in his interpretation, the treaty only referred to property (slaves) at the time of its signing on November 29, 1782. The evacuated Blacks had been granted freedom prior to that date, he said. To appease Washington, he said he would keep a record of the names and descriptions of Blacks on the British ships in case his interpretation was overruled and compensation was ordered. The result was a 150-page, handwritten Book of Negroes that cataloged three thousand people relocated to Nova Scotia. It recorded the name, age, physical description, and status (slave or free) for each Black passenger, including one of Washington's own escaped slaves, Harry. Also on board a departing ship were Banastre Tarleton's British Legion of loyalist troops.

Parker and other Americans looking for slaves in New York were only able to return a small number to their owners. Children who were not born behind British lines were separated from their parents and returned to slavery. Most Blacks were secure on British military and other vessels that the American "commissioners," glorified slave catchers, were not permitted to search. Blacks constituted about 10 percent of the Royal Navy in New York, and they just sailed away.

Life was so difficult for Black loyalists in Nova Scotia that close to 1,200, including Harry Washington, jumped at the opportunity to resettle in a new British colony in Sierra Leone in 1792. The settlement in Sierra Leone was funded by English abolitionists. Banastre Tarleton was not among the British with high-minded motives. His family profited from the Liverpool-based slave-trading business, and he was famously proslavery, even mocking English abolitionists such as William Wilberforce after the Revolutionary War.

Cassandra Pybus estimated that close to nine thousand runaway slaves had left America as free people by the final evacuation on November 23, 1783. There is no record of what happened to the many thousands of other runaways. Many were returned to slavery. Many may have found freedom in Northern states. Six of Washington's slaves had gone missing.

Today, the story of the 1783 Black settlement in Birchtown, Nova Scotia, is remembered as the Black Loyalist Heritage Centre. "For the past two decades, we, the descendants of the founding settlers have proudly celebrated our story of the Black Loyalists and have tenaciously worked to preserve our cultural identity through planning and research," the group states on its website.

At his death, Morgan had sixteen slaves on his farm in Virginia, possibly including the two he had taken as human booty at Cowpens.

Following the Revolutionary War, Morgan organized and led a group of militia to southwestern Pennsylvania to combat the Whiskey Rebellion. He served one term in the House of Representatives and died in 1802. He was an American military hero, but he has been mostly forgotten. In 1790, Congress struck a gold medal to honor Morgan for his victory at Cowpens. One of his homes, Soldier's Rest, near Berryville, Virginia, is a privately owned registered historic landmark. A monument was erected in his honor in Spartanburg, South Carolina, in 1881 to mark the centennial of the Battle of Cowpens.

Books about Morgan have odd factual contradictions. Was he or was he not a teamster present at the Battle of the Monongahela? Some writers assume he was at the battle because he was employed in Braddock's baggage train. But it's possible, if not likely, that he was in a supply group that was not present at the battle. Books differ on when and where he was whipped for punching a British officer unconscious. Writers often penned adoring biographies of Morgan that minimized the warts.

But one historian, Vaughn Scribner, of the University of Central Arkansas, took a very dark view of Morgan: "Morgan's life was indeed an 'outline' for white men's success in an America defined by unfreedoms and inequality: he killed and displaced Native Americans for his extensive land-holdings in the Ohio Valley region; exploited the labor and firepower of African Americans in his bid for military prowess and genteel status; and continuously negotiated mercurial lines of hierarchy, gender, and honor during his scrabble to the top of Virginia's powerful gentry."[40]

I asked Lawrence Babits his opinion of this view. His response, "This statement is a 'neopolitically correct view.'" He added, "One thing to keep in mind with all past events is that in their time, these

---

[40] Vaughn Scribner, review of *Daniel Morgan: A Revolutionary Life*, by Albert Louis Zambone, *Journal of Southern History* 85, no. 4 (2019).

were ways that things were done. Applying more recent, and often politically/emotionally charged, viewpoints isn't really fair to the people who acted in roles that history gave them."

Tarleton also has a complicated role in American memory.

If Americans know of him at all, it is probably from the 2000 Mel Gibson movie called *The Patriot*, in which the British Legion is portrayed as green-helmeted thugs and rapists. Their leader is a colonel named William Tavington, who gathers townspeople in a house and then burns it down. Mel Gibson movies, such as *Braveheart*, are infamous as caricatures of history. Tarleton gets even worse treatment in a television show called *Sleepy Hollow*, where he is portrayed as a demon who is a sadistic torturer. A fan site says the portrayal "is possibly worse than his real-world counterpart." No doubt.

Mel Gibson movies and Fox TV shows are not proxies for real history, but for most people, particularly children, that's the only exposure they have to historical figures, such as Tarleton or Scottish nationalist William Wallace, the subject of Mel Gibson's *Braveheart*.

An English author named M. S. Morgan, upset by Tarleton's American portrayal, tried to set the record straight with a 2020 book called *The Case for the Defence of Banastre Tarleton: A British assessment of Lt. Colonel Banastre Tarleton in the American War of Independence*. He wrote, "Tarleton was in fact, one of the most deadly, proficient, and capable officers on the British side who took hundreds of prisoners. This alone made him hated by the Americans and their propaganda machine. In truth, the Patriots needed a form of monster, an anti-Christ with whom they could identify and scare the people into submission. Tarleton was the British ogre, what the fight was all about—deposing the demonic monsters from England."

To those who are still passionate about the Revolutionary War from the British perspective, Banastre Tarleton is, in a slight sense, their version of Nathan Bedford Forrest, the Confederate cavalry leader covered in chapter 5. Both were generally very successful, and they attacked the enemy in a courageous and dashing style. They were brutal at times. Troops led by both were said to have led massacres of soldiers who had surrendered. Both have an association with slave trading. Defenders of their actions say they should not be judged by today's politically correct standards.

British author Morgan does not question that British troops committed atrocities in the South. Cornwallis ordered British officer James Wemyss to treat rebels "in the most rigid manner." Weymss burned homes and hanged opponents. The war in the South was a brutal civil war pitting loyalists against rebels. There was ugliness on both sides. Sometimes the loyalist excess misfired, driving men into the militia.

For the record, Tarleton was a far different person from Forrest. He attended Oxford, while Forrest had almost no formal education. Tarleton went on to a successful political career in England after the war, while Forrest became a leader of the Ku Klux Klan.

Tarleton defender M. S. Morgan wrote, "At a time when many in Britain questioned the war and its point after the defeat at Saratoga in 1777, Banastre Tarleton gave them victories and hope." The same applies to Forrest. He provided good news for Southerners, even though many of his actions were little more than guerilla raids on a very extended Union supply chain.

Unlike Forrest in the South, Tarleton was not memorialized in England.

"Even in his home city today, there is very little trace of him and even less acknowledgement of his service in the military and as a member of the British parliament," wrote Morgan, referring to Liverpool, England. "There is more of a Confederate presence in Liverpool than of Tarleton," Babits said.[41]

Babits also told me this about Tarleton: "His treatment of opponents on the battle was no different from that of American Continental dragoons as can be seen with [Henry] Lee's treatment of the loyalist detachment he destroyed in Pyles Hacking Match in North Carolina or [William] Washington's destruction of a Tory force at Hammond's Store in South Carolina in the fortnight before Cowpens. Dragoons were supposed to be ruthless, and cavalry was essential in providing intelligence and keeping would-be participants cowed enough so they would opt out of joining up. So in that

---

[41] Lawrence Babits, communication with author, July 17, 2021.

sense, I wouldn't say Tarleton's behavior was much different from the American dragoon officers'. His press reputation was pretty bad in terms of rebel American propaganda and subsequent writings by Whig authors after the war. Mel Gibson's movie *The Patriot* is a generic copy of those Whig postwar writings."

Daniel Morgan and Banastre Tarleton provide interesting examples of how we remember historical figures. We exaggerate the deeds of our own military leaders while ignoring their faults. We also inflate—sometimes ridiculously—the evils of our opponents.

In reference to the Battle of Cowpens, what was its historical significance? To Lieutenant Colonel John Moncure of the US Army Command and General Staff College, "Cowpens may be one of the most important battles ever fought on American soil from the standpoint of the tactical lessons one can learn from it."

Morgan knew the British were beatable using the right tactics. He knew the British were overconfident and susceptible to a frontier battle approach. Morgan understood, anticipated, and then planned for the battle tendencies of his soldiers. He planned perfectly for the possibility that local militia would cave under pressure. Robert Dunkerly commented, "Morgan certainly DID trust his militia: he knew how to use them, he knew their strengths and weaknesses and positioned them so as to succeed."[42]

He also knew and trusted the steadiness of his regular infantry. Some commanders might have panicked when troops failed to properly execute an order to refuse a line. He realized quickly after meeting with Howard that the troops were confused, not panicking. He took command and led the troops into a rare double envelopment of the enemy. It wasn't part of his original plan, but when he saw the opportunity, he seized it. As a result, initiative was taken from a better-trained and better-equipped force.

Morgan said he was outnumbered by Tarleton, but that has been a source of controversy. An estimate of about 1,150 for Tarleton's forces is not contested.

---

[42] Robert Dunkerly, email to author, July 15, 2021.

A study of Cowpens by Moncure put Morgan's strength at 350 for the Continental Line, 750 for the militia, and 72 for the cavalry. Ed Bearss, who helped design the Cowpens site in 1967, estimated the militia line at 300. Princeton historian Allen Guelzo put Morgan's total force at 800. Everyone seems to have different numbers.

Babits brought science to the discussion. Based on his research of various records and use of extrapolation, Babits estimated Morgan's forces at about two thousand. Babits told me, "To work up the North Carolina, South Carolina, and Georgia militia numbers, I relied on a large number of pensions, some muster rolls, personal accounts, and statistical projections." In 2015, Babits participated in an archaeological project that covered the militia line from one end to the other. "Its distance over the ground is barely enough space for a thousand men," he added.

In his after-action report, Morgan seemed to anticipate a controversy over his troop strength. Two days following the battle, Morgan wrote to Greene, "From our forces being composed of such a variety of corps, a wrong judgment may be formed of our numbers. We fought only 800 men, two-thirds of which were militia." A federal monument at the battlefield lists Morgan's total force at 970.

My look at pension applications did make it clear that a few men did show up at the last minute, very possibly escaping Morgan's attention.

One was nineteen-year-old Samuel Sexton. He said he had been beaten by Tories, escaped, and headed to Cowpens to join the militia. "On my route to the Cowpens, I succeeded in inducing 25 men to join me, and was chosen their captain." He arrived at Cowpens the day before the battle, and his group joined Pickens's line of militia.[43]

Morgan was not familiar with these men. But some, such as a Georgia militia group, had a significant war record. The mounted sentries, or videttes, that first detected Tarleton's approach were commanded by Joshua Inman, captain of a group of backwoods fighters unofficially called the Georgia Refugees.

---

[43] Moncure, 100. Reprinted from Revolutionary War Pension Applications, September 17, 1833.

In *The Journal of the American Revolution*, Wayne Lynch wrote, "No official regiment known as the Georgia Refugees ever existed. When government in Georgia collapsed, these men simply refused to surrender and carried on as an insurgency." They are rarely included in reports of Cowpens, or elsewhere, for that matter. They don't fit into that neat image of how we want to be remembered. Lynch said the Georgia Refugees used "brutal tactics of murder and intimidation that Americans would actually like to avoid knowing much about."[44]

Cowpens was designated a national battlefield in 1972, and today it is a beautiful space. A one-mile loop trail starts behind the visitors center and heads down the old Green River Road, which split both armies. You walk past signs noting Morgan's three lines. The meadow that divided the two armies at dawn is being restored to its condition in 1781, a large grassy area with a few hardwood trees and cane. Signs on the loop back note key events, such as where the Continental Line reformed after confusion over an order. The National Park Service keeps it simple and clear. There are only two monuments on the battlefield: one built in 1932 by the US government and one erected in 1856 by the Washington Light Infantry of Charleston, South Carolina.

Cowpens is a largely forgotten battle outside of military training manuals, yet it speaks loudly about how America became a nation and how we remember the past.

---

[44] Wayne Lynch, "Victory for the Georgia Refugees," *Journal of the American Revolution*, September 29, 2014.

CHAPTER 4

Oliver Hazard Perry and the Battle of Lake Erie

The last roar of cannon that died along the shores of Lake Erie was the expiring note of British domination.

—Washington Irving

A 352-foot-tall monument towers above the picturesque resort town of Put-in-Bay, Ohio, located on an island in Lake Erie. The monument honors an American victory fought in 1813 seven miles to the west in the little-remembered War of 1812. In 2019, a reviewer on Trip Adviser wrote, "I don't really know what happened in the War, however, the views from the monument are awesome!"

The monument also commemorates peace between Britain, Canada, and the United States since 1815. The United States and Canada today have the longest undefended border in the world. At one time, the border was on fire.

The War of 1812 usually gets cursory treatment in history classes. New England states voted against war. The British burned the White House. Andrew Jackson won a famous battle at New Orleans eighteen days after the war officially ended. In 1815, a treaty was signed that mostly maintained the status quo.

Perry's Victory and International Peace Memorial in Put-in-Bay, Ohio. The Canadian, United Kingdom, and United States (circa 1812) flags are flown at the same height. (Wikimedia Commons by Christopher Graft)

One event not generally remembered is the Battle of Lake Erie, in which a squadron led by Oliver Hazard Perry captured or sank a roughly equivalent British squadron on September 10, 1813. The flagships for both fleets were built from scratch close to Lake Erie as both sides raced preparations for a battle. Perry was victorious despite insubordination—and possibly cowardice—from his second-in-command. He overcame a shellacking at the beginning of the battle, and his battle flag, "Don't Give Up the Ship," became an American naval icon, even though he gave up his ship.

The cause of the War of 1812 was a lack of respect for American sovereignty. In order to man its huge navy, Britain seized sailors from merchant ships. Thomas Jefferson listed impressment as one of the British crimes in the Declaration of Independence, but the practice didn't stop after the Revolutionary War.[45] In fact, it escalated during the Napoleonic Wars. More than half of Britain's 120,000-strong Royal Navy in 1805 had been taken by press gangs from several countries.

Between 1789 and 1815, it's estimated that the British impressed more than nine thousand Americans.[46]

The seizures from America's merchant fleet triggered outrage among war hawks, who wanted to take possession of Canada in retaliation. The committee on foreign relations in the US House of Representatives stated, "Seeing in the measures adopted by Great Britain, a course commenced and persisted in, which must lead to a loss of national character and independence, feel no hesitation in advising resistance by force."

In a drive spearheaded by Speaker Henry Clay of Kentucky, the House passed its first-ever war resolution in a largely sectional vote of 79 to 49. On June 18, 1812, President James Madison signed a Declaration of War. The size of the national army at the outbreak of the war was just 6,744.

Madison told the states to raise one hundred thousand militiamen, including fourteen thousand from Pennsylvania. The New England states, which opposed the war, ignored the directive. Pennsylvania had sixteen militia divisions, including General David Mead's Sixteenth Pennsylvania Militia, and he had the authority to raise troops from seven counties in northwestern Pennsylvania. And he did so on multiple occasions to defend ships under construction in Erie.

The war was fought at first along the Canadian frontier. Native Americans led by Tecumseh quickly joined the British side in Detroit. Tecumseh led a tribal confederation that had been fighting to retain control of their land west of the Allegheny Mountains since the end

---

[45] Daniel James Ennis, *Enter the Press-gang: Naval Impressment in Eighteenth-Century British Literature* (Newark, Delaware: University of Delaware Press, 2002), 170.
[46] John Deeban, "The War of 1812: Stoking the Fires," *Prologue* 44, no. 2 (Summer 2012), National Archives, https://www.archives.gov/publications/prologue/2012/summer/1812-impressment.html.

of the Revolutionary War. Their most recent adversary was Indiana Territory governor, and future president, William Henry Harrison, who had angered the Natives with what they considered bogus treaties taking their land.

Early in the war, the United States failed in attempts to invade Canada and lost Detroit and Chicago. The British improved a naval base near Detroit and took control of navigation on Lake Erie, stranding a force of several hundred soldiers led by Harrison in northwestern Ohio. Harrison, whose defensive bases in Ohio had been attacked by combined forces of British and Native Americans, was anxious for naval support so he could retake Detroit.

The Navy Department was ordered "to obtain command of the Lakes Ontario and Erie, with the least possible delay." The assignment to build necessary vessels went to Isaac Chauncey, commandant of the Brooklyn Navy Yard. Hundreds of sailors and shipwrights were transferred to a naval base at Sackets Harbor, New York, on Lake Ontario.

On October 7, 1812, Madison wrote to General Henry Dearborn: "The command of the lakes, by a superior force on the water, ought to have been a fundamental point in the national policy, from the moment peace took place [1783]."[47]

A key player in the effort to regain control of Lake Erie was Daniel Dobbins, a resident of Erie whose trading ship was seized by the British at the outbreak of the war. He was briefly held prisoner, and after his release, he met in Washington, DC, with Madison and Secretary of Navy Paul Hamilton. Dobbins recommended construction of a fleet at Erie, citing its protected harbor at Presque Isle Bay and access to timber. Erie, however, had a population under five hundred and no manufacturing. The bay was partially blocked by a sandbar.

---

[47] "From James Madison to Henry Dearborn, 7 October 1812," Founders Online, National Archives, https://founders.archives.gov/documents/Madison/03-05-02-0280. (Original source: *The Papers of James Madison*, Presidential Series, vol. 5, July 10, 1812–February 7, 1813, eds. J. C. A. Stagg, Martha J. King, Ellen J. Barber, Anne Mandeville Colony, Angela Kreider, and Jewel L. Spangler [Charlottesville: University of Virginia Press, 2004], 371–373.)

Dobbins was named a sailing master in the US Navy and told to take the first steps to build four gunboats to US Naval specifications in Erie. He immediately adapted the design to meet the challenging sailing requirements of Lake Erie, where sudden storms can wreak havoc because of the lake's relatively shallow depth. Eugene Ware, an author and local student of Dobbins, wrote, "The innovative design had a higher freeboard, wider beams, and were rigged with much more extensive and square sails. The ship's guns were moved to midship and away from the bow to give better balance to the ship and add speed while under sail."[48]

The wisdom of building boats in the town's harbor was questioned by the senior naval commander on Lake Erie. Lieutenant Jesse Elliot, of the Black Rock naval base, wrote on October 2, 1812, "It appears to me utterly impossible to build gunboats at Presqu'ile; there is not a sufficient depth of water on the bar to get them into the lake. Should there be water, the place is at all times open to the attacks of the enemy, and in all probability when ready for action will ultimately fall into the hands of the enemy."[49]

Dobbins, however, overrode the objections, feeling boats could be moved over the sandbar, which had a six-foot clearance at normal lake depth at that time. Plus, there were no other harbors on the lake. The Black Rock naval station was located on the Niagara River near Buffalo and was within gun range of British Forts Erie and George.

Construction began in November 1812 on the gunboats. Two months later, the new Great Lakes naval commodore, Chauncey, hired a Brooklyn Navy Yard shipwright named Noah Brown to take charge of the construction of two brig-rigged corvettes, the *Niagara* and the *Lawrence*, at Erie. *Brig-rigged* means "two-masted, square-sailed ships." Corvettes are the smallest class of naval warships.

---

[48] Eugene Ware, "Who Was Daniel Dobbins?" GoErie.com, May 15, 2020, https://www.goerie.com/news/20200515/who-was-daniel-dobbins-----eries-mystery-hero.

[49] Laura Sanford, *The History of Erie County, Pennsylvania, from Its First Settlement* (self-published, 1894), 242.

The race was on to finish construction of the boats before ice on the lake melted. Security remained an issue. On March 14, Dobbins wrote to the secretary of the Navy: "I find I cannot raise any volunteers to guard the vessels, but have made arrangements with the carpenters in the yard to stand guard."[50]

A race was also underway to build a British fleet at the Amherstburg Royal Naval Dockyard on the Detroit River in Ontario. Facilities included a storehouse, two blockhouses, a timber yard, and a wharf. To the north of the naval yard was Fort Malden, built by the British in 1795 to defend against a possible American invasion. Four ships were built in the yard, which received most of its supplies via Lake Erie—a route soon to be challenged by Perry's squadron. Also in the English squadron were three vessels converted to warships and a small US brig, *Adam*, captured when Detroit fell.

In February 1813, Chauncey requested that the secretary of the Navy appoint Oliver Hazard Perry as commander of the Erie squadron, a job he badly wanted. Perry, a twenty-seven-year-old Navy officer commanding a flotilla of gunboats in Newport, Rhode Island, had asked for transfer to the Great Lakes, writing to Chauncey, "On the first prospect of a declaration of war, I hastened to Washington in the hope of obtaining active employment; but, unfortunately, there was no vacancy. The honourable secretary of the navy, however, promised me the first one that should occur suitable to my rank; none has occurred until the present. I therefore hope, sir, I may be gratified in being appointed to the Argus [a Great Lakes brig]."[51] Perry also asked Rhode Island senator Jeremiah B. Howell to intercede on his behalf.

Perry, who was born in South Kingston, Rhode Island, in 1785, had commanded the sloop-of-war *Revenge* from 1809 to 1811. After his appointment was granted, he was told to bring one hundred men from Newport to beef up the very shorthanded crew in Erie. He traveled from Buffalo to Erie on a lake ice sleigh in late March. His

---

[50] Ibid., 245.
[51] Alexander Mackenzie, *Commodore Oliver Hazard Perry: Famous American Naval Hero, Victor of the Battle of Lake Erie, His Life and Achievements* (New York: D. M. MacLellan Book Company, 1910), 91.

appointment may have irked Lieutenant Jesse Elliot, who had been in charge of Lake Erie naval operations and was senior in rank to Perry prior to February 1813. His opinion on boat building at Erie had earlier been overridden.

In another critical decision made by Chauncey, the *Lawrence* and the *Niagara* would be armed with thirty-seven thirty-two-pounder carronades, specially designed naval artillery that shattered wooden hulls at short range. In an article for the Naval Historical Foundation, retired rear admiral Denys W. Knoll wrote, "At short range [one-half mile] it had a crushing effect more destructive than the swift passage of a ball from guns designed for longer ranges [two miles] which threw shot at higher velocities… One great advantage of the carronade was that it made traverse [right or left] firing possible."

Perry's first project was to shore up the shipbuilding effort in Erie and acquire necessary supplies. He traveled to Pittsburgh for iron, ordered canvas from Philadelphia, and personally supervised mechanics who made hardware for the vessels. Captain A. K. Wooley supervised casting of the shot.

The carronades were produced at the Columbia foundry owned by George Foxall in Washington, DC. Fourteen wagons carried the carronades to Pittsburgh, possibly using some of the same route taken by Braddock's army in 1755. The trip took more than a month. Other guns were transferred from Sackets Harbor.

One of Perry's biggest worries was security. On April 16, he wrote to General Mead: "I am at this moment informed that power is vested in you to call out the militia for the defense of this place. You doubtless are acquainted that there is a number of vessels of war building here, and that there is no force to protect them. The Navigation is now nearly open between this and Malden [British fort near Detroit] and from the importance to the enemy to destroy those vessels, we may confidently expect they will attempt it. Should they succeed it will be an everlasting disgrace to the country as well as an irremediable loss. If you feel yourself at liberty to order on one hundred men, it would in my opinion add much to our security."

Mead answered the call for militia then and several more times, depleting manpower in nearby farming communities.

Three gunboats were launched and equipped in early May 1813. The two five-hundred-ton brigs each equipped with twenty guns were ready in late May. The brig *Lawrence* was named for Captain James Lawrence, who was mortally wounded June 1 in a naval battle outside Boston. His last words, "Don't give up the ship," were used by Perry on his battle flag. The *Lawrence* was launched from dry dock in late June, and the brig *Niagara* a few days later.

Commanding the British fleet near Detroit was Robert Heriot Barclay, a veteran of the Trafalgar campaign in 1805. His initial command included seven British seamen, 108 provincial Marines, fifty-four Royal Newfoundland fencibles (militia), and 106 soldiers in the Forty-First Regiment of Foot. His fighting strength would rise to the 440-to-490 range. Barclay raced to complete construction of a new flagship, the HMS *Detroit*. Ships on both sides were made with green timber. There was no time to let the wood age. No matter, one boatbuilder said, they'd only be in one fight.

Even though the carronades were developed by the Carron Co. of Scotland, none were available for the *Detroit*. It was equipped with twenty-seven land guns with long barrels from Fort Malden. "No warship ever had a more unsuitable battery," commented Rear Admiral Knoll in his analysis of the battle.

The guns dictated the basic strategies for each side. Perry wanted to get the *Lawrence* and the *Niagara* close to the *Detroit* and then shoot it out. Barclay wanted to blast the American brigs with the *Detroit*'s long guns before they could get close. Wind direction, which was often in flux on Lake Erie, would be critical to Perry's strategy. Both Barclay and Perry pleaded for reinforcements, particularly experienced seamen.

Barclay's six-ship squadron blockaded Presque Isle on July 20 but then lifted the blockade July 30 to return to Detroit for supplies. Perry again appealed to Mead. This time he also wanted help from the militia to move his fleet over the sandbar so he could engage Barclay.

Mead issued a call to arms: "Your state is invaded. The enemy has arrived at Erie threatening to destroy our navy and the town. His course, hitherto marked with rapine and fire wherever he touched our shore, must be arrested. The cries of infants and women, of the aged and infirm, the devoted victims of the enemy and his savage allies, call on you for defense and protection. Your honor, your property all require you to march immediately to the scene of action. Arms and ammunition will be furnished to those who have none, at the place of rendezvous near to Erie and every exertion will be made for your subsistence and accommodation."[52]

Mead stationed 230 members of his newly recruited 136th and 137th Regiments of the Sixteenth Division Militia near the boatyard. Many of them only served for two or three weeks in July and August in 1813, according to pay receipts in the Library of Congress.[53] Total pay for most of the noncommissioned officers and privates was $5 to $7.

Many militiamen were older. Early militia volunteers were posted elsewhere. Young men were needed to work the farms. One member of the militia was seventy-year-old Sergeant Aaron Wright, who lived on a four-hundred-acre farm awarded for his service as a rifleman in the Revolutionary War. Also present in the defense of the boatyard was Wright's son-in-law Corporal James Mumford, whose farm was adjacent to Wright's.[54]

On August 7, he again appealed to Mead for militia to help lift the ships over the sandbar and provide protection for this particularly vulnerable moment, and Mead summoned men for their farms and 230 assisted.[55]

---

[52] Herbert Bell, *History of Venango County, Pennsylvania: Its Past and Present* (Venango, Pennsylvania: Brown, Runk & Company, 1890), 269.

[53] Library of Congress, "Expenditures by the State of Pennsylvania on Behalf of the United States, 1812–1814," https://www.loc.gov/resource/dcmsiabooks.expendituresbyst00unse/?sp=162&r=0.088,0.898,0.637,0.358,0.

[54] Ibid.

[55] Daniel H. Hanes, "The Life and Times of a Western Pennsylvania Militia Musket," paper presented to the Ohio Gun Collectors Association, March 10–11, 2018, Wilmington, Ohio, 10, https://www.ogca.com/Spring%20NL%202018%20for%20web.pdf.

Perry began—with great effort—to move his ships out of the harbor. Brown had designed the two bigger ships with nine-foot drafts and developed a system using flotation tanks, or camels, to lift them over the sandbar. He needed to gain roughly three feet of clearance. Camels, which fit on both sides of the ship's hull, were sunk to the ship's portholes, and then water was pumped out, lifting the ship. The process took two days. The shallow-draft gunboats cleared the sandbar with little problem.

Perry was reinforced with seventy much-needed sailors led by Jesse Elliott, the same officer who had earlier criticized Erie as a boat-building location. Another fifty reinforcements arrived from the USS *Constitution*, which was being refitted in Boston after its engagements, including defeat of the HMS *Guerriere*. Barclay returned to reimpose a blockade, but Perry had boats in the lake. Barclay withdrew to Detroit, where workers were finishing the *Detroit*.

Perry moved west to engage Barclay and sheltered at Put-in-Bay, an island near Harrison's base in northwestern Ohio. Frontier riflemen from Harrison's force were added to act as sharpshooters and marines. Both sides were short on supplies, but Barclay's situation was more critical since Perry now controlled navigation on the lake.

Battle of Lake Erie
Order of Battle

US Navy
Oliver Hazard Perry, commander (on the *Lawrence*)
Jesse Elliott, commander (on the *Niagara*)
531 sailors and soldiers, 54 guns
Flagship *Lawrence*, 18 32-pounders and 2 long 12-pounders
Niagara, 18 32-pounders (also called carronades) and 2 long 12-pounders

Caledonia, 3 three long 12-pounders
Ariel, six, 4 long 12-pounders
Trippe, 1 long 32-pounder
Tigress, 1 long 32-pounder
Somers, 1 long 24 and one long 12-pounder
Scorpion, 1 long 24 and one long 12-pounder
Porcupine, 1 long 32-pounder.

Royal Navy
Robert Heriot Barclay, commander
440 to 490 sailors and soldiers, 63 guns
Flagship *Detroit*, 1 24-pounder carronade, 1 18-pounder carronade, 2 24-pounder long guns, 1 18-pounder long gun (on a pivot), 6 12-pounder long guns, and 8 9-pounder long guns
Queen Charlotte, 14 24-pounder carronades, 1 24-pounder long gun (on a pivot), and 2 24-pounder long guns
Lady Prevost
Chippewa
Hunter
Little Belt

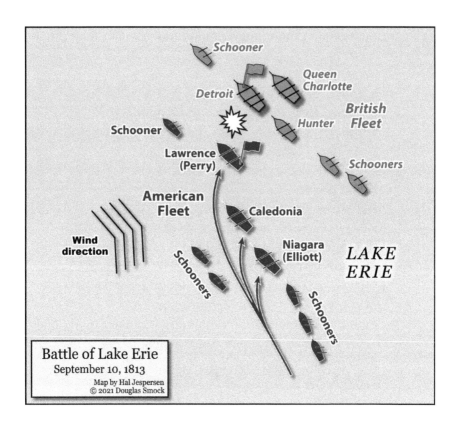

The battle formation favored the Americans, but Perry's flagship was quickly destroyed while the Niagara held back.

On September 10, Barclay's six ships approached Put-in-Bay. Perry's group moved out and formed a line of battle. The Americans had more vessels, but the Royal Navy had more cannons. The number of combatants was roughly equal. The British commander was a combat veteran who had served with Vice Admiral Horatio Nelson. The American fleet had a fluttering wind in its sails. Knowing he had the wind and the initiative, Perry met with his officers and laid down his line of battle and order of attack. The commander of each vessel was assigned a British vessel to attack.

The battle began with Barclay lining up his fleet on port tack position in a close column so that each ship had support if attacked by the *Niagara* or the *Lawrence*. They were, from front to rear, *Chippewa, Detroit, Hunter, Queen Charlotte, Lady Prevost*, and *Little Belt*. On a port tack, wind was blowing over the ships' left side, a position providing poor maneuverability.

With a view of the British line, Perry modified his plan of attack. He led with the *Scorpion* and the *Ariel*, followed by the *Lawrence, Caledonia, Niagara*, and then four schooners. Shortly before noon, a band on the British flagship struck up "Rule, Britannia!" and then fired her long guns at the Lawrence. The *Scorpion* and the *Ariel* returned fire with their long guns.

Perry ordered each vessel to fire upon its designated opponent and pulled the *Lawrence* to within 250 yards of the *Detroit*. She turned to the wind and opened fire with her carronade battery. The *Queen Charlotte* sailed past the *Hunter* and opened fire with its carronades on the *Lawrence*. Much of the rigging on Perry's flagship was soon in tatters from a withering fire.

At this point, with the *Lawrence* under disabling fire, the *Niagara* failed to engage the *Queen Charlotte* as directed in Perry's order of attack. Its commander, Jesse Elliott, said he was obeying Perry's order to maintain a line of battle. Some of Perry's men later accused Elliott of cowardice, and this was one of the battle's long-debated arguments.

Naval officer and historian Alfred Thayer Mahan wrote, "Elliott's place therefore was alongside the Queen Charlotte, so to engage her that she could attend to nothing else. This he did not do… There is little reason for doubt that the tenor of Perry's instructions required Elliott to follow the Queen Charlotte, and no doubt whatever that military propriety imperiously demanded it of him."[56]

One issue in dispute was the strength of the wind between noon and 2:00 p.m. Was it strong enough for Elliott to move the *Niagara* into position?

After two, Elliott moved the *Niagara* into the battle. At this point the *Lawrence* and the *Detroit* were both badly damaged. More

---

[56] Alfred Thayer Mahan, *Sea Power in Its Relations to the War of 1812*, vol. 2 (Cambridge, United Kingdom: Cambridge University Press, 2011), 68.

than half of the *Lawrence*'s crew were dead or wounded. Only one gun was functional. But her colors still flew. Barclay was severely wounded, and his first lieutenant was dead. The captain of the *Queen Charlotte* was dead, and her second-in-command was knocked senseless. The *Lady Provost*, fifth in line, had a broken rudder.

Perry departed the *Lawrence* in its first cutter (workboat) with a few hands and headed to the *Niagara*. The *Lawrence* surrendered after Perry boarded the *Niagara* and quickly took command, moving her to the *Detroit*. The *Detroit* and the *Queen Charlotte* became entangled, making them sitting ducks for the *Niagara*, which was joined in the attack by smaller vessels in Perry's fleet.

Then in the words of the officer now commanding the *Detroit*, "The ship lying completely unmanageable, every brace cut away, the mizzen-topmast and gaff down, all the other masts badly wounded, not a stay left forward, hull shattered very much, a number of guns disabled, and the enemy's squadron raking both ships ahead and astern, none of our own in a position to support us, I was under the painful necessity of answering the enemy to say we had struck (surrendered), the Queen Charlotte having previously done so."[57]

There were forty-one killed, ninety-four wounded on the British side, and twenty-seven killed, ninety-six wounded on the American side. It was a rare surrender of an entire British squadron. Barclay faced a court-martial and was found innocent. Perry was widely acclaimed, but there was considerable acrimony regarding Elliott. Perry commended Elliott in his official report, but in language that Elliott deemed equivocating. Subordinates of Perry's—over his objections—publicly questioned Elliot's actions. Elliott challenged Perry to a duel, which he refused.

In 1818, Perry filed six courts-martial charges against Elliott with Secretary of the Navy Benjamin W. Crowninshield. The first three dealt with Elliot's action after the battle. The next three dealt with dereliction of duty during the battle. Perry withdrew the charges under pressure, and possibly in exchange for the title of commodore. In 1819, Perry died of yellow fever.

---

[57] Ibid., 72.

After studying all the charges and countercharges, historian David Curtis Skaggs weighed in against Elliott with this assessment of the controversy: "In the final analysis, great subordinates in naval engagements show initiative and follow the commander's intent, if not his explicit instructions, when the changing circumstances of battle warrant it."

The battle was written about by amateur historian and future president Theodore Roosevelt, who took a unique view[58]; eminent US Navy scholar Alfred Thayer Mahan; and even novelist-turned-historian James Fennimore Cooper, whose account of the battle relied heavily on official reports and triggered a whole new round of back-and-forth.

In Roosevelt's analysis of the battle, the Americans had a significant advantage in firepower and were clear favorites to win. In *The Naval War of 1812*, he wrote, "The important fact was that though we had nine guns less, yet, at a broadside, they threw half as much metal again as those of our antagonist. With such odds in our favor it would have been a disgrace to have been beaten." Firepower is measured as the weight of shot discharged at a broadside, or nearly simultaneous firing of all the guns from one side of a warship.

In Roosevelt's view, Perry deserved plaudits for his work building the fleet at Erie, not for his victory in the Battle of Lake Erie. "Captain Perry showed indomitable pluck, and readiness to adapt himself to circumstances; but his claim to fame rests much less on his actual victory than on the way in which he prepared the fleet that was to win it. Here his energy and activity deserve all praise, not only for his success in collecting sailors and vessels and in building the two brigs, but above all for the manner in which he succeeded in getting them out on the lake."

Roosevelt said the War of 1812 offered a lesson in preparedness. "The subject merits a closer scrutiny than it has received. At present people are beginning to realize that it is folly for the great English-

---

[58] Meredith Hindley, "Roosevelt the Revisionist," *Humanities* 34, no. 5 (September/October 2013), https://www.neh.gov/humanities/2013/septemberoctober/feature/roosevelt-the-revisionist.

speaking Republic to rely for defence upon a navy composed partly of antiquated hulks, and partly of new vessels rather more worthless than the old," he wrote in 1882. He became assistant secretary of the Navy fifteen years later and became president in 1901. The Navy was strengthened under his watch, culminating in the projection of US naval power in a global tour from 1907 to 1909 of sixteen battleships known as the Great White Fleet.

Perry's Victory on Lake Erie, painted by William Henry Powell, shows Oliver Hazard Perry's transfer from the Lawrence to the Niagara. It now hangs in the Ohio statehouse. (Public domain)

Perry's victory secured Lake Erie and Detroit. Immediately after Perry's victory, British troops in Detroit commanded by Major General Henry Procter retreated eighty miles northeast via the Thames River to Moraviantown, Ontario. They were followed by the British tribal allies under Tecumseh. After Perry's fleet transported

Harrison's forces across Lake Erie, they drove off the British and then defeated the tribal confederacy, killing Tecumseh.

On October 22, Perry wrote to Mead, "It may be some satisfaction to your deserving corps to be informed that you did not leave your harvest fields, in August last, for the defense of this place without cause." A document in Procter's baggage disclosed a plan to attack Erie in August "beyond doubt." It was thwarted by a lack of military manpower needed to overtake the guarded shipyard.[59]

But the war took a turn for the worse after Napoleon abdicated in 1814 and Britain could focus on the American front. British troops burned the Capitol, and the war ended in 1814. Although the Treaty of Ghent made no significant changes, the war had important consequences. Perry's victory combined with the victories of Benjamin Harrison's land forces subdued the Native Americans, and settlers were safer in continuing their westward movement. Indiana was admitted to the Union in 1816, followed by Illinois in 1818. Canada gradually moved away from British control and became independent in 1867.

Importantly, the United States established itself on more equal footing with European superpowers. Rear Admiral Knoll wrote, "It took the War of 1812 to secure for us the full recognition and respect of world powers for our rights and privileges as a sovereign nation. The War of 1812 also firmly established our present northern border with Canada. It ended for all time British claims to certain territories in our country and the subsequent withdrawal of British troops from those territories."

The War of 1812 is little studied and little remembered in the United States today.

Perry's battle flag hangs at the US Naval Academy in Annapolis, Maryland. His battle slogan, "Don't Give Up the Ship," remains sacred in the Navy. In the 1970s, a class of guided-missile frigates was named after Perry. In 2015, Rhode Island, in honor of its native

---

[59] Spencer Mead, *History and Genealogy of the Mead Family of Fairfield County, Connecticut, Eastern New York, Western Vermont, and Western Pennsylvania, from AD 1180 to 1900* (Knickerbocker Press, 1901), 44–45. Google Books.

son, launched the SSV *Oliver Hazard Perry*, described as the largest civilian sailing school vessel in the United States.

The new brig Niagara under sail on Lake Erie.
(Wikimedia Commons, by Lance Woodworth)

In addition to a National Park Service museum in Put-in-Bay, Ohio, the Erie Maritime Museum in Erie commemorates the shipbuilding and the battle. A reconstructed Niagara is berthed nearby and is still actively used for sailing instruction. The relief flagship replica preserves the art of historic square-rig seamanship.

Henry Foxall, whose foundry produced carronades for the *Lawrence* and the *Niagara*, had promised that if Perry won, he would build a church. Called the Foundry Chapel, it was built in Washington, DC, soon after the war ended. It was rebuilt a few blocks away in 1904 and is now called the Foundry United Methodist Church. President Bill Clinton and Hillary Clinton were members.

One of the most significant memories of the War of 1812 is a very silent one. When I walk through old Pennsylvania cemeteries within one hundred miles of Erie, it's amazing how many graves sport War of 1812 veterans' markers. In the *History of Erie County, Pennsylvania*, Samuel P. Bates wrote, "There were few able-bodied male residents of the county who were not obliged to serve in the militia at some time during the war. The alarms were sent over the country by runners, who went from house to house stirring up the inhabitants. It happened more than once that whole townships were nearly depopulated by their male citizens."

I feel a solemnity when I walk through the Peterson Cemetery in Cochranton, Pennsylvania, and see flags flying next to militiamen's graves. The cemetery is located way back in the woods on a dirt road that locals need to point out.

The militia in the Battle of Lake Erie got little respect, echoing themes from the Battle of Cowpens and George Washington's first Virginia militia. Historians usually note the role of General David Mead but include no information on the militia. One exception was the book *Flames Across the Border: The Canadian-American Tragedy, 1813–1814* by French Canadian historian Pierre Berton. He wrote that the Erie guards "were a comic opera regiment of Pennsylvania militia who were too afraid of the dark to stand watch at night." They were the Rodney Dangerfields (a comic who got no respect) of the American military. But they got the job done. The ships were safely built and lifted over the sandbar.

America's recollection of the War of 1812 is a quiet one. Americans don't want to remember that we invaded Canada, or that the British burned our Capitol. It also brings back our country's sad history with indigenous peoples.

The war came back into public view briefly on January 6, 2021, when supporters of President Donald J. Trump stormed congressional offices. Newscasters noted that it was only the second breach of those halls in American history. The first time was by a foreign invader. The second time was by our own citizens brandishing misappropriated historical flags in what they proclaimed as an act of patriotism.

CHAPTER 5

Nathan Bedford Forrest and the Fort Pillow Massacre

A certain moment arrived when Forrest's men were no longer fighting a battle in a war between civilized nations. They were from that moment on sharing in a race riot, a mass lynching.

—Carl Sandburg,
American poet and biographer

Everywhere, it seemed, I had to explore two pasts and two presents; one white, one black, separate and unreconcilable. The past had poisoned the present and the present, in turn, now poisoned remembrance of things past.

—Tony Horwitz,
Confederates in the Attic: Dispatches from the Unfinished Civil War

Some people view Confederate cavalry leader Nathan Bedford Forrest as a man of honor, courage, and chivalry. To others, he is a racist butcher. Does he represent the best or the worst of the old South? There is a new focus on Forrest because of Black activism and a harder reckoning with American history. A key event determining his legacy was a brief battle in which the fatality rate for Black Union soldiers was double that of Whites. Despite congressional hearings, sworn depositions, official military reports, and many personal accounts, the facts of what happened remain in dispute and clarity is still only slowly emerging from an emotional historical haze.

From a military perspective, Forrest's 1864 attack on the small riverside garrison at Fort Pillow, Tennessee, was not a consequential event in the Civil War. It was highly controversial at that time but faded in American memory. It's significant today for its role in Black memory. It's also important as a lens for examining what place Forrest holds—and deserves—in American memory.

The General Nathan Bedford Forrest Historical Society, headquartered in Memphis, Tennessee, historically held an annual Forrest Valentine Confederate Ball with music from the Fifty-Second Regimental String Band, "1860s period attire recommended." The group's website states, "The PURPOSE of the Society is to honor and preserve the name and heroic deeds of General N. B. Forrest and his Cavalry."[60]

That glory was respectable to the likes of Southern novelist and historical writer Shelby Foote, who said that "Forrest is one of the most attractive men who ever walked through the pages of history."[61] Forrest permeates the work of Nobel Prize–winning novelist William Faulkner, who wrote a story in 1943 titled *My Grandmother Millard and General Bedford Forrest and the Battle of Harrykin Creek*.[62]

In *The Saddest Words: William Faulkner's Civil War*, Professor Michael Gorra wrote, "Forrest is the one Rebel general who stands for Faulkner as more than a name. The novelist mentions him in a half dozen books, seeing him as a kind of trickster, forever sowing confusion and counting coup (engaging in brave acts in battle) on

---

[60] The General Nathan Bedford Forrest Historical Society, http://www.tennessee-scv.org/ForrestHistSociety/.

[61] Carter Coleman, Donald Faulkner, and William Kennedy, "Shelby Foote, the Art of Fiction No. 158," *The Paris Review*, no. 151 (Summer 1999), https://www.theparisreview.org/interviews/931/the-art-of-fiction-no-158-shelby-foote.

[62] William Faulkner, "My Grandmother Millard and General Bedford Forrest and the Battle of Harrykin Creek," https://faulkner.drupal.shanti.virginia.edu/content/my-grandmother-millard-and-general-bedford-forrest-and-battle-harrykin-creek.

a clumsy enemy." Faulkner even believed, probably falsely, that one of his ancestors served under Forrest. Forrest biographer Brian Steel Wills wrote, "For Faulkner, Bedford Forrest represented the ambiguity—the unique mixture of honor and curse, fantasy and reality—of the Southern experience."

Nathan Bedford Forrest Memorial in Live Oak Cemetery in Selma, Alabama. (Wikimedia Commons)

Forrest was a key figure with Lost Cause writers, who denied the existence of a massacre at Fort Pillow, let alone any culpability on Forrest's part. His biographers mythologized his life, stoking the legend that still lingers. Forrest and his cavalries rode like men on fire throughout the Civil War protecting Tennesseans and Mississippians from the Yankees. Many Tennesseans still celebrate Forrest's birthday on July 13, but Forrest's legacy is significantly harder to defend than the legacy of other Confederate heroes, such as Robert E. Lee or Stonewall Jackson.

Forrest's cavalry butchered African American Union soldiers, as well as White soldiers, who had surrendered at Fort Pillow in 1864. The Fort Pillow massacre goes down with the My Lai massacre in Vietnam as two of the darkest moments in American military history.

Although Confederates, including Forrest, incorporated Black slaves into their army as personal attendants and laborers, they were enraged when Abraham Lincoln freed slaves in the Confederate states and then enlisted them in the Union Army as soldiers. By the end of the war, 209,145 Blacks accounted for about 10 percent of the Union Army. About 20 percent of African American soldiers died, a rate that was 35 percent higher than the rate for White US troops. Sixteen received the Medal of Honor. They gave the depleted armies of Ulysses S. Grant fresh energy and a large numerical majority. They fought with intensity and passion that surprised some White officers. Many proudly displayed "Remember Fort Pillow" pennants, patches, or hat bands.

Before the war, Forrest was a slave trader. After the war, he became a leader of the Ku Klux Klan. He was born in 1821 in a rural town about forty miles south of Nashville. His dad was a blacksmith who moved the family to a humble farm in northern Mississippi in 1834 and died three years later, leaving Forrest as primary breadwinner for the family. When his mother planned to marry, he became a trader in livestock and people. In 1851, he relocated to Memphis, where he made a fortune in the slave trade as slavery was migrating to the newly developing, cotton-growing Mississippi Delta region.

From 1814 to 1840, the federal government made large acquisitions of territory from Native Americans east of the Mississippi River, significantly expanding land for cotton growing. The Treaty of Old

Town with the Chickasaw in 1818 opened up western Tennessee. Cotton production in the counties around Memphis went from zero in 1800 to more than fifty thousand bales each in 1860. Slave populations in the southwestern counties of Tennessee went from negligible in 1800 to more than ten thousand each in 1860. The legal Atlantic slave trade ended in 1808, but a new mass migration began from the old tobacco farms on the Eastern Seaboard to the burgeoning cotton fields farther west and south. Close to one million slaves were moved.[63]

Much of Forrest's profits from the slave trade were reinvested in real estate, including a plantation in Mississippi with thirty-six slaves. In the 1860 census, Forrest valued his properties at $190,000 in addition to personal holdings of $90,000, roughly equivalent to more than $8 million today. He had only a few months of formal education, no military training, and no military experience. His profile was far different from those of most Civil War commanders, who usually had Mexican War experience, West Point or other military institute training, or political position and the ability to recruit troops. What Forrest had were money, courage, love for the South, and a thirst for combat.

In June 1861, he joined a Tennessee cavalry company as a private but was quickly commissioned a lieutenant colonel by the governor of Tennessee and recruited five hundred men. He bought pistols, saddles, and other equipment in neutral Kentucky and smuggled them back to Memphis. He quickly became embroiled in the fast-moving war in Tennessee. Much of his personal fortune was spent on equipping many hundreds of soldiers he recruited into the Confederate cavalry.

The Union had a formidable strategy, called the Anaconda Plan. The Confederacy would be choked by a coastal blockade coupled with control of the Mississippi River. Henry Halleck, commander of the newly created US Department of Missouri, told Grant to attack vulnerable Confederate forts on the Cumberland and Tennessee Rivers. A squadron of gunboats commanded by Andrew H. Foote captured Fort Henry on the Tennessee River on February 6, 1862. Ten days later, Foote and Grant captured Fort Donelson on the Cumberland River. The

---

[63] Edward Baptist, *The Half Has Never Been Told*, (New York: Basic Books, 2014), 40, table 1.1. Overdrive E-Book.

next stop for the Union Army was Pittsburg Landing on the Tennessee River, where Generals Ulysses S. Grant and William T. Sherman won the Battle of Shiloh in early April after being surprised and initially overwhelmed by a Confederate Army. The next domino was Corinth, Mississippi, an important rail hub, which fell in May. A Union fleet captured New Orleans in late April. The commander of Confederate-held Fort Pillow, located forty miles north of Memphis on the eastern side of the Mississippi River, was told to abandon the fort when prudent.

In the battles at Fort Donelson and Shiloh, Forrest, the newly commissioned cavalry officer, urged senior commanders to pursue aggressive tactics. They chose to surrender at Fort Donelson but allowed Forrest and his men to make an overnight escape. At Shiloh, General P. T. Beauregard had little choice but to retreat, directing Forrest to protect his rear on April 7, 1862. At a place now known as Fallen Timbers, he led a charge into Union infantry, was surrounded, shot, and then escaped. He grabbed a Union soldier to cover his back while he galloped away, dropping the soldier later.

The loss at Shiloh was a stunning early defeat for the Confederacy. Lost Cause champions felt that Beauregard's failure to press an attack at the end of the first day was a fatal error. If only Forrest had been in charge, some felt, the battle might have been won; the Confederacy might have been saved.

The reality was far different. Standing on Grant's final line at Pittsburg Landing on a spring day in 2021 and looking down a steep ravine to a creek, I could envision Beauregard's difficulty as darkness fell after the first day of fighting, Confederates were exhausted and running low on ammunition. Rebels attacked Grant's hilltop line until about 8:00 p.m. and were blown back by blistering rifle and cannon fire. A few federals, expecting a night attack, dug breastworks. Grant was urged by several staff to regroup on the other side of the Tennessee River. "'Not beaten yet by a damn sight," he famously muttered and stormed back the next day. The Lost Cause proponents were correct that Shiloh was very important. They were wrong that a cavalry officer with no military training and little experience could have won the day for the Confederates. Forrest's judgment was not respected by Confederate commanders, with whom he would tangle throughout the war. He spent most of the war fighting in military backwaters because of his poor ability to take orders and fit into the structure of a large army.

Forrest prided himself for fighting in a "civilized" manner, but issues began to crop up in 1862 after he was given a new cavalry command with orders to slow the advance of a Union Army toward Chattanooga, Tennessee. There were reports that Forrest murdered a captured Black servant to a Union officer. Forrest biographer Wills commented, "There can be no doubt that the participation of Blacks in the Union war effort angered [Forrest]. And he was certainly not averse to expressing that anger in a personal and violent manner."

Separately, General Braxton Bragg told Forrest to form another new command with fresh recruits. Bragg viewed Forrest as a semi-independent raider who excelled at recruiting. He was also very good at equipping his new commands with guns, ammunition, clothing, food, and other supplies taken from the Union in lightning-like raids.

After Union forces captured Fort Donelson, Foote moved his gunboats back to the Mississippi River. Supported by the Union Army of the Mississippi commanded by Brigadier General John Pope, Foote captured a Confederate stronghold at Island Number Ten on the Mississippi River on April 8, 1862. The river was now clear to Fort Pillow, the last line of defense before Memphis. The fort had been upgraded in 1861 under the supervision of Confederate brigadier general Gideon Johnson Pillow, who used as many as 1,500 slaves to dig the earthworks. Its purpose was to stop a Union invasion down the Mississippi and at one time was armed with fifty-eight cannons.

On May 10, the Confederate River Defense Fleet attacked Union ships near Fort Pillow. Although Foote's *Cincinnati* was sunk and the *Mound City* badly damaged, the Confederates evacuated the fort. The Stars and Stripes was hoisted June 5, and Union gunboats proceeded downriver and attacked Memphis. According to newspaper accounts, slaves gathered on the riverbanks to cheer the gunboats as they passed.

The Union Army established a garrison at Fort Pillow in September to police far western Tennessee, which had erupted into cruel guerilla warfare. Runaway slaves sought shelter in the fort, and some were hired as cooks and servants. A trading post was established on the riverbank. The legal status of runaway slaves in the Confederate states was confusing from a Union perspective. President Abraham Lincoln was trying to build as broad a coalition as possible to wage the war and was slow to issue the Emancipation Proclamation. The coalition included Democrats who supported slavery and border states where slavery was still practiced. There was no prohibition of slavery in the US Constitution, so runaways who sought shelter behind Union lines were considered contraband or property captured from an enemy. Many escaping slaves in the Fort Pillow area were sent to a contraband camp at Island Number 10. In July 1862 the US Militia Act decreed that Blacks could join the Union Army. Abraham Lincoln's Emancipation Proclamation freed more than 3.5 million slaves in the Confederacy as of January 1, 1863, accelerating recruitment into the newly formed United States Colored Troops (USCT). The new troops were often assigned to garrison duty.

"All members of the new Black units faced great hostility from the Confederacy," wrote historian John Cimprich. "Concerned about both property rights and the specter of slave rebellion, the Confederate Congress refused to recognize Blacks as soldiers and left it to state authorities either to return captured ones to owners or to execute them as insurrectionaries." In May 1863, the Union Army began enlisting runaway slaves at Fort Pillow.

In late 1862 and early 1863, Forrest led raids against Union forces in Tennessee and captured a Union raiding party in Alabama led by Colonel Abel Streight. His quick temper led to a fight with a subordinate, who was mortally wounded. Forrest participated in the Battle of Chickamauga in September 1863 and was angered when Bragg assigned his cavalry to a different commander because of Forrest's insubordination. Forrest accosted his commanding officer, calling him a coward and unworthy of a duel. That would have been grounds for serious disciplinary action in most armies, but Forrest was on his way to becoming a living legend. Confederate president Jefferson Davis intervened and granted Forrest permission to operate semi-independently in western Tennessee and northern Mississippi and then promoted him to major general. Forrest's main objective was to tie up Union troops so they could not be used in the offensive against Chattanooga. For the remainder of the war, Union commanders such as Sherman were glad that Forrest was detached to the West.

In February, 1864, as Forrest was preparing to recruit fresh rebel troops in western Tennessee and Kentucky, fresh Union troops from Tennessee moved into Fort Pillow. The new Thirteenth Tennessee Cavalry was commanded by Major William T. Bradford. Next in was a detachment of the Second US Colored Light Artillery, recently organized from contrabands and others. Bradford's orders were to fight local guerillas, improve the fort, and continue recruiting. The fort sheltered runaway slaves, rebel deserters, and Union sympathizers who had been harassed by secessionists. An armed wooden steamship called the *New Era* was stationed nearby. Forrest was active in the area, and Fort Pillow was reinforced with a detachment from the First Battalion of the Sixth US Colored Heavy Artillery commanded by Major Lionel F. Booth, who was senior and became commanding officer. The fort now had six cannons and almost 600 soldiers: 295 White and 262 Black troops. More could be dispatched to the fort by ship in case of an attack. The troops were very green and lightly trained. More than 60 men in Bradford's unit were former Confederate soldiers, according to historian Gregory Macaluso. Forrest's new recruits had their own problems; many were deserters from the Confederate infantry. Not long after the battle at Fort Pillow, many were arrested and returned to their commanders, according to Brian Steel Wills.

Fort Pillow Order of Battle

US Army, Fort Pillow Garrison
557
Major Lionel F. Booth, commanding, killed during the battle
Major William F. Bradford, assumed command

6th Regiment Colored Heavy Artillery: Major Lionel F. Booth
13th Tennessee Cavalry: Major William F. Bradford
2nd Regiment, Colored Light Artillery, Company D: 2nd Lieutenant Daniel Van Horn
USS *New Era*, 157-ton gunboat with 6 24-pounder howitzers: Acting Master James Marshall

Confederate States of America, Forrest's Cavalry
1,500
Major General Nathan Bedford Forrest, commanding
Captain Charles W. Anderson, aide-de-camp (led 200 men to Forrest's left flank)
Brigadier General James R. Chalmers, commanding at the beginning of the battle
Colonel Robert A. (Red Bob) McCulloch's Brigade (of Chalmers' Division)
—2nd Missouri Cavalry: Robert (Black Bob) McCulloch
—Willis's Texas Cavalry Battalion: Lieutenant Colonel Leonidas M. Willis
—8th Mississippi Cavalry: Lieutenant Colonel William L. Duff
—18th MississippI, Mississippi Partisan Rangers: Lieutenant Colonel Alexander Chalmers
—5th Mississippi Cavalry: Lieutenant Colonel Wiley B. Reed
—McDonald's 3rd Tennessee Cavalry Battalion: Lieutenant Colonel J. M. Crews
Fourth Brigade, General Tyree H. Bell
—22nd Tennessee Cavalry (also called the 2nd Tennessee): Colonel Clark R. Barteau

—21st Tennessee Cavalry (also known as 16th Tennessee): Colonel Andrew N. Wilson
—15th (or 20th) Tennessee Cavalry: Colonel Robert M. Russell
—18th (or 19th) Tennessee Cavalry: Colonel John F. Newsom
Hoole's Company, Mississippi Light Artillery: Captain Edwin S. Walton (4 guns, including howitzers; gained and operated 6 additional guns in the battle)

Note: The Confederate units had multiple designations because of reorganizations. Over time, some were remembered after the name of an early commander, such as McDonald's Tennessee Cavalry. Many lacked official recognition because of the chaotic nature of the war. Barteau's Second/Twenty-Second Tennessee Cavalry Regiment was not official because its commander was captured before his orders of organization were filed with the Confederate War Department. No appointments were made to the regiment from the War Department. In April 1863, Andrew N. Wilson was authorized to raise a new command in West Tennessee in federal territory, but his Twenty-First/Sixteenth Cavalry was never officially recognized by the Adjutant and Inspector General's Office.

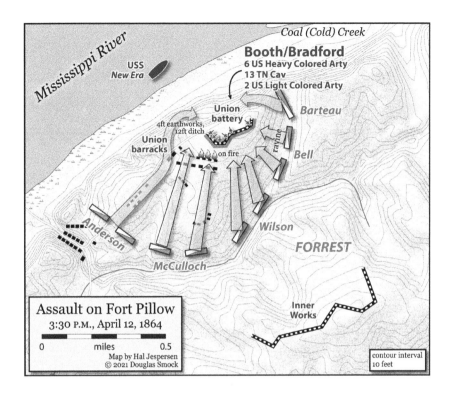

The map shows Confederate positions just before the final assault on the fort. Troops under Barteau and Anderson were at the back of the fort, cutting off retreat. Some had cut through ravines to the river landing, setting up the massacre that followed.

Forrest decided to attack the fort to capture horses and supplies. Angered by reports of atrocities, he probably also wanted to punish the Tennessee troops fighting for the Union. There is no reason to believe that Forrest attacked the fort with intent to massacre Black soldiers. On the rebel side, there were 1,500 Cavalry troops commanded by Forrest, who directed Brigadier General James R. Chalmers to open the attack on April 12, 1864.

In an after-action report, Forrest described the fort like this: "The fort is an earth-work, crescent shaped, is 8 feet in height and 4 feet across the top, surrounded by a ditch 6 feet deep and 12 feet in width, walls sloping to the ditch but perpendicular inside. It was garrisoned by 700 troops with six pieces of field artillery. A deep ravine surrounds the fort, and from the fort to the ravine the ground descends rapidly."

Following is an official report of the battle written by Lieutenant Mack J. Leaming of the Tennessee cavalry in a deposition requested by US secretary of war Edwin Stanton: "At 5:30 o'clock on the morning of the 12th of April, 1864, our pickets were attacked and driven in by the advance of the enemy, under command of Gen. Forrest. Our garrison immediately opened fire on the advancing rebels from our artillery at the fort, while Companies D and E, of the Thirteenth West Tennessee Cavalry, were deployed as skirmishers, which duty they performed until about 8 am, when they were compelled to retire to the fort after considerable loss, in which Lt. Barr of Company D was killed."

Leaming added, "The firing continued without cessation, principally from behind logs, stumps, and under cover of thick underbrush and from high knolls, until about 9 am, when the rebels made a general assault on our works, which was successfully repulsed with severe loss to them and but slight loss to our garrison. We, however, suffered pretty severely in the loss of commissioned officers by the unerring aim of the rebel sharpshooters, and among this loss I have to record the name of our post commander, Maj. L. F. Booth, who was killed almost instantly by a musket-ball through the breast.

"Maj. W. F. Bradford, of the Thirteenth West Tennessee Volunteer Cavalry, being the next ranking officer, then assumed command of the garrison and directed the remainder of our operations. At about 11 am the rebels made a second determined assault on our works. In this attempt they were again successfully repulsed with severe loss. The enemy succeeded, however, in obtaining possession of two rows of barracks running parallel to the south side of the fort and distant about 150 yards. The barracks had previously been ordered to be destroyed, but after severe loss on our part in the attempt to execute the order our men were compelled to retire without accomplishing the desired end, save only to the row nearest to the fort. From these barracks the enemy kept up a murderous fire on our men, despite all our efforts to dislodge him.

"Owing to the close proximity of these buildings to the fort, and to the fact that they were on considerably lower ground, our artillery could not be sufficiently depressed to destroy them, or even render them untenable for the enemy. Musketry and artillery firing continued, however, on both sides with great energy, and although our garrison was almost completely surrounded, all attempts of the enemy to carry our works by assault were successfully repulsed, notwithstanding his great superiority in numbers."

A southbound Union ship, the *Liberty*, had stopped to pick up civilians fleeing the battle and proceeded to Memphis to sound the alarm for reinforcements. The *New Era* gunboat provided defensive fire from the Mississippi River. Forrest halted firing when ammunition ran low. After supply wagons arrived in midafternoon, Forrest sent a truce party, offering no terms. Forrest offered to treat the surrendering Union troops as "prisoners of war," which was more generous than offers he had made in similar situations.[64] Bradford refused to surrender.

Forrest originally offered the Union officers an hour to respond to his offer of truce but spied reinforcements arriving by riverboat. He reduced the time to twenty minutes and still received no for an answer. He ordered an assault after moving to the back. The fort was taken in twenty minutes, and the riverboat retreated under fire.

Lieutenant Leaming's report continued, "During the cessation of firing on both sides, in consequence of the flag of truce offered by the enemy, and while the attention of both officers and men was naturally directed to the south side of the fort where the communications were being received and answered, Forrest had resorted to means the most foul and infamous ever adopted in the most barbarous ages of the world for the accomplishment of his design. Here he took occasion to move his troops, partially under cover of a ravine and thick underbrush, into the very position he had been fighting to obtain throughout the entire engagement, up to 3:30 p.m. Consequently, when the final decision of the garrison had been made known, the rebel charge was immediately sounded; when, as if rising from out the very earth on the center and north side, within 20 yards of our works, the rebels received our first fire, wavered, rallied again and finally succeeded in breaking our lines, and in thus gaining possession of the fort. At this juncture, one

---

[64] Brian Steel Wills, email to author, September 1, 2021.

company of the Sixth US Heavy Artillery, colored troops, rushed down the bluff, at the summit of which were our works, and many of them jumped into the river, throwing away their arms as they fled.

"Seeing that through a gross violation of the rules of civilized warfare the enemy had now gained possession of our works, and in consequence that it would be useless to offer further resistance, our men threw down their arms and surrendered. For a moment the fire seemed to slacken. The scene which followed, however, beggars all description. The enemy carried our works at about 4 p.m., and from that time until dark, and at intervals throughout the night, our men were shot down without mercy and almost without regard to color. This horrid work of butchery did not cease even with the night of murder, but was renewed again the next morning, when numbers of our wounded were basely murdered after a long night of pain and suffering on the field where they had fought so bravely."

Forrest's cavalrymen hated not just the freed Blacks who had become soldiers; they also hated the Tennesseans who had fought for the Union.

Lieutenant Leaming, the highest-ranking Union officer to survive the battle, continued, "The rebels were very bitter against these loyal Tennesseans, terming them 'home-made Yankees,' and declaring they would give them no better treatment than they dealt out to the negro troops with whom they were fighting." He estimated that at least 300 of the Union dead were not killed in fighting; they were murdered. Total Union dead were around 450. The death rate for Black soldiers was double the rate for Whites, which included 13 officers of Black troops.[65]

During the attack, Forrest had suffered painful injuries. The *New Era* had fired 282 rounds of shell, shrapnel, and canister into the Confederate lines, which also received fire from the fort's artillery. The Confederate cavalry leader, who liked to be close to the action, was struck twice, once by a spent canister, and again by a piece of timber propelled by an exploding shell. His determination to remount new horses and fight on inspired his troops.

---

[65] John Cimprich, *Fort Pillow, a Civil War Massacre, and Public Memory* (Baton Rouge, Louisiana: Louisiana State University Press, 2005), 85.

In his final assessment, Union Lieutenant Leaming told federal investigators, "The bravery of our troops in the defense of Fort Pillow, I think, cannot be questioned. Many of the men, and particularly the colored soldiers, had never before been under fire; yet every man did his duty with a courage and determined resolution, seldom if ever surpassed in similar engagements. Had Forrest not violated the rules of civilized warfare in taking advantage of the flag of truce in the manner I have mentioned in another part of this report, I am confident we could have held the fort against all his assaults during the day."

A reconstructed inner fort at a Tennessee State Historical Park shows the trench taken by the Confederates and cannon positions. The slope of the earthworks is not as steep as first-person accounts indicated.

Leaming's allegation that Confederate troops moved into a critical position during the truce was confirmed in the autobiography of Confederate captain John W. Carroll. He wrote, "While the flag of truce was up Captain James Stinnett and I with some picked men crawled up close under the guns to be ready in case they refused to surrender to prevent them from discharging their cannon into our ranks which we successfully did."[66]

Another confirmation came from Charles Robinson, a civilian photographer from Minnesota who donned a blue blouse and grabbed a gun when the attack commenced. Describing what happened during the truce, he wrote home on April 17, "The Rebels took advantage of this, and crawled on their hands & knees into the trenches, so that when the flag of truce went back they had gained an advantage which they could not have done had we not recognized the flag."[67]

Also supporting the story was Daniel Van Horn, second lieutenant, Company D, Sixth US Heavy Artillery (Colored), who wrote, "During the time consumed by this consultation, advantage was taken by the enemy to place in position his force, they crawling up to the fort."[68]

Leaming said he was seriously wounded after the surrender and was offered aid by a Confederate officer.

In a separate report on the battle, two other Union cavalry lieutenants added these details: "We saw several Negroes burning up in their quarters on [the next] morning. We also saw the rebels come back that morning and shoot at the wounded. We also saw them at a distance running about, hunting up wounded, that they might shoot them. There were some whites also burning… Major Anderson, Forrest's assistant adjutant-general, stated that they did not consider colored men as soldiers, but as property, and as such, being used by our people, they had destroyed them. This was concurred in by Forrest, Chalmers, and McCulloch, and other officers."

---

[66] John W. Carroll, *Autobiography and Reminiscences of John W. Carroll*, electronic edition (Academic Affairs Library, University of North Carolina at Chapel Hill, 1996), https://docsouth.unc.edu/fpn/carroll/carroll.xml.

[67] George Bodnia, ed., "Fort Pillow 'Massacre': Observations of a Minnesotan," Minnesota History 43, no. 5 (Spring 1973), 188–190, http://collections.mnhs.org/MNHistoryMagazine/articles/43/v43i05p186-190.pdf.

[68] Daniel Van Horn, Sixth US Colored Heavy Artillery, report of the capture of Fort Pillow, https://civilwarhome.com/vanhornftpillowor.html.

Robinson's letter home added further detail: "As soon as the rebels got to the top of the bank there commenced the most horrible slaughter that could possibly be conceived. Our boys when they saw that they were overpowered threw down their arms and held up, some their handkerchiefs & some their hands in token of surrender, but no sooner were they seen than they were shot down, & if one shot failed to kill them the bayonet or revolver did not. I lay behind a high log & could see our poor fellows bleeding and hear them cry 'surrender' 'I surrender' but they surrendered in vain for the rebels now ran down the bank and putting their revolvers right to their heads would blow out their brains or lift them up on bayonets and throw them headlong into the river below."

Forrest's after-action report summed up the battle like this: "Assuming command, I ordered General Chalmers to advance his lines and gain position on the slope, where our men would be perfectly protected from the heavy fire of artillery and musketry, as the enemy could not depress their pieces so as to rake the slopes, nor could they fire on them with small-arms except by mounting the breast-works and exposing themselves to the fire of our sharpshooters, who, under cover of stumps and logs, forced them to keep down inside the works. After several hours' hard fighting the desired position was gained, not, however, without considerable loss. Our main line was now within an average distance of 100 yards from the fort, and extended from Coal Creek, on the right, to the bluff, or bank, of the Mississippi River on the left. During the entire morning the gunboat kept up a continued fire in all directions, but without effect, and being confident of my ability, to take the fort by assault, and desiring to prevent further loss of life, I sent, under flag of truce, a demand for the unconditional surrender of the garrison."

A Union surgeon named Charles Fitch witnessed the slaughter and sought protection from Forrest, who was in the fort helping to line up a captured Parrott gun on the *New Era*. Forrest told him, "You are the surgeon of a damn nigger regiment." Forrest spared the surgeon's life after he said he was assigned to the White troops and was not from Tennessee. Forrest maintained that he stopped his soldiers from shooting Union troops, who allegedly had continued to return fire while retreating down the embankment. In his analysis of the battle, Andrew Ward wrote in *River Run Red*, "It is possible that as Forrest headed for the Parrott gun, he may have issued an order to halt the slaughter in the fort itself. But if so, it was ignored, and as he and his Escort fired at the New Era, Forrest did nothing to stop the slaughter below, much of which was being carried out in his name and well within his view."[69]

Forrest captured six pieces of artillery, two ten-pounder Parrotts (rifled artillery), two twelve-pounder howitzers, and two brass six-pounder guns, and about 350 small arms. He reported the capture of "164 Federals, 75 Negro troops, and about 40 Negro women and children." The women and children had sought shelter in the fort.

In another report on the battle, Forrest said, "The river was dyed with the blood of the slaughtered for two hundred yards. The approximate loss was upward of five hundred killed, but few of the officers escaping. My loss was about twenty killed. It is hoped that these facts will demonstrate to the Northern people that Negro soldiers cannot cope with Southerners."

A US naval officer who arrived the following morning was allowed by Forrest to bury the dead and evacuate the wounded. He wrote this in his report of what he saw: "Of course, when a work is carried by assault there will always be more or less bloodshed, even when all resistance has ceased; but here there were unmistakable evidences of a massacre carried on long after."

For some people, Forrest's failure was that he lost control of his men, not that he led them in the barbarity. The issue was debated for more than one hundred years, but in the view of Professor Michael Gorra, the question is now settled: "A letter home by a Confederate sergeant, written immediately afterward but not fully published until 1982, tells of soldiers shot as they tried to surrender, with the general himself ordering the 'butchery' to continue."[70]

---

[69] Andrew Ward, *River Run Red: The Fort Pillow Massacre in the American Civil War* (New York: Viking Adul, 2005), 230–231.

[70] Michael Gorra, *The Saddest Words: William Faulkner's Civil War* (New York: Liveright Publishing, 2020), 214.

The letter was written two days after the battle by Sergeant Achilles V. Clark of the Confederate Twentieth Tennessee Cavalry. He wrote, "The slaughter was awful. Words cannot describe the scene. The poor deluded negros would run up to our men fall on their knees and with uplifted hands scream for mercy but they were ordered to their feet and then shot down. The white men fared but little better. The fort turned out to be a great slaughter pen. Blood, human blood stood about in pools and brains could have been gathered up in any quantity. I with several others tried to stop the butchery and at one time had partially succeeded but Gen. Forrest ordered them shot down like dogs and the carnage continued. Finally our men became sick of blood and the firing ceased."[71]

In his memoirs, General Ulysses S. Grant wrote that "Forrest made a report in which he left out the part which shocks humanity to read."

Another view came from Sherman, now theater commander for the Union, who wrote, "The massacre at Fort Pillow occurred April 12, 1864, and has been the subject of congressional inquiry. No doubt Forrest's men acted like a set of barbarians, shooting down the helpless negro garrison after the fort was in their possession; but I am told that Forrest personally disclaims any active participation in the assault, and that he stopped the firing as soon as he could. I also take it for granted that Forrest did not lead the assault in person, and consequently that he was to the rear, out of sight if not of hearing at the time, and I was told by hundreds of our men, who were at various times prisoners in Forrest's possession, that he was usually very kind to them. He had a desperate set of fellows under him, and at that very time there is no doubt the feeling of the Southern people was fearfully savage on this very point of our making soldiers out of their late slaves, and Forrest may have shared the feeling."

Forrest felt he had been treated unfairly by sensational newspaper reports in the North and highly politicized congressional hearings. "I'm also aware that I am at this moment regarded in large communities of the North with abhorrence as a detestable monster, ruthless and

---

[71] Brooks D. Simpson, ed., *The Civil War: The Final Year, Told by Those Who Lived It* (2013), 42–44.

swift to take life and guilty of unpardonable crimes with the capture or Fort Pillow." He said that congressional testimony on the massacre was based on leading questions. Some writers strongly supported Forrest as a man of great character and emphasized Union soldiers' refusal to surrender, taunting, and alleged drinking as reasons for their deaths.

At the end of the war, Forrest refused entreaties to continue a guerilla war. He told his men to become good citizens, and he returned to his plantation in Mississippi, paying former slaves for their work. Union officers assisted in assembling his work crew. There was another troubling incident in 1866 when he was found not guilty of manslaughter after he killed one of his freedmen in a fight.

His life remained haunted by Fort Pillow as some Republicans pushed for further investigation. Confederate veterans looked to him for leadership and elected him the first grand wizard of the Ku Klux Klan after its founding, according to members. Forrest later denied he even belonged to the KKK but wrote of his efforts to suppress its violence. Historian Wills weighed in: "If he did not actually command the Ku Klux Klan, Bedford Forrest certainly acted like a commander… Under Forrest's control, the Ku Klux Klan became a major force of counterrevolution in Tennessee and the rest of the South." President Andrew Johnson pardoned him for his Confederate service on July 17, 1868, and he died in 1877.

The debate about Forrest and Fort Pillow remains active. Some of Forrest's modern defenders are willing to accept that a massacre did occur at Fort Pillow, but they will not accept that he ordered or even condoned the murder of Black soldiers. Like crack defense attorneys, they attack the evidence. Congressional hearings that implicated Forrest in a massacre were biased and politicized. There were holes in the sworn testimony of Union witnesses who named Forrest. Much of the testimony was hearsay. Confederate sergeant Achilles Clark did not say that he saw Forrest directly. Northern newspapers exaggerated events. Forrest was unfairly persecuted.

Another argument by Forrest's defenders is that he valued Blacks as property and wanted them returned to their owners, not murdered. He said that in later conversations defending his role at Fort Pillow.

But did he ever make that clear to his troops? Forrest demanded 100 percent obedience from his command. They did what they thought he wanted. The slaughter extended into the night. Would that have happened if Forrest had issued a clear order to stop?

There were several layers of possible culpability for Forrest. Did he order his troops to murder Black soldiers? Did he look the other way after the massacre started? Was he totally oblivious to what was happening around him? People will believe what they want to believe. Historian Brian Steel Wills summed up his view of Forrest's culpability this way: "Bedford Forrest was not innocent of the blood shed at Fort Pillow anymore than he was responsible for designing or executing a deliberate massacre there."

Frank Leslie wood engraving shows Confederates massacring Union soldiers after they surrender at Fort Pillow. (New York Public Library Digital Collections)

What happened at Fort Pillow was not isolated. There were reports of Black soldiers being murdered by Confederates after they surrendered in other battles. A little more than three months later, Black soldiers were killed after they attempted to surrender in the disastrous Battle of the Crater during Grant's siege of Petersburg, Virginia. The death toll of Black soldiers was 439, even more than those who died at Fort Pillow. "The murder of surrendered Black troops at Fort Pillow was part of a demonstrable pattern of Confederate behavior," wrote University of Virginia professor Elizabeth R. Varon in her 2019 book *Armies of Deliverance: A New History of the Civil War.*

The sacrifices of the Black soldiers spurred the US Army to appoint more Black officers and boost their pay to the same as White soldiers'. Pension inequities for widows of dead Black soldiers were addressed after a personal appeal to President Lincoln by Lizzie Booth, the widow of the Fort Pillow commander. In a final irony, in March 1865 the desperately shorthanded Confederacy enacted legislation permitting recruitment of Black soldiers.

Forrest was a complicated man. He believed in honor, but he was a racist with a violent temper. People like Shelby Foote and William Faulkner could separate the good Forrest from the bad Forrest.

Greg Mertz, a retired National Park Service historian, explained to me why he thought figures such as Faulkner and Foote admired Forrest: "When military groups take staff rides of the Fredericksburg and Chancellorsville, Virginia Civil War battlefields, their leaders said their goal is to figure out how the US armed forces can produce more soldiers like the successful Confederate generals Robert E. Lee and Thomas J. 'Stonewall' Jackson, and fewer soldiers like the unsuccessful Union opposing generals Ambrose E. Burnside and Joseph Hooker. The recent military has been able to encourage soldiers to emulate the talents of these great generals on the field of battle while still separating that from other aspects of their lives, including decisions to fight against the United States and supporting a Confederate cause that perpetuated the institution of slavery.

"Foote and Faulkner admired the military genius of Forrest, who campaigned on their home turf of Tennessee and Mississippi.

No other Confederate general in the West achieved a higher degree of military success than Forrest.

"Among Shelby Foote's contributions to the Ken Burns documentary was the sharing of his belief that America committed two great sins—slavery and the manner in which it ended slavery. Such a view is not consistent with someone who would admire Forrest's occupation as a slave trader or as someone playing a significant role in the Ku Klux Klan. Foote and Faulkner were able to do as the recent military has done and separate an admiration for Forrest's achievements while in the saddle as a cavalry leader, with those aspects of his life for which they disapproved and would not wish to emulate."[72]

In an essay in *The Atlantic* magazine in 2011 titled "The Convenient Suspension of Disbelief," Black novelist Ta-Nehisi Coates said, "There are many lies here," after quoting Foote's view of the Southern cause. Coates said that Foote idolized Lee and Forrest with great words, yet "Black southerners like Harriet Tubman, Andrew Jackson Smith or Robert Smalls are met with no such laurels."

Coates said he enjoyed reading Foote's trilogy of the Civil War immortalized in Ken Burns's *The Civil War* series on PBS, yet he added, "Shelby Foote wrote the Civil War, but he never understood it. Understanding the Civil War was a luxury his whiteness could ill-afford."[73]

Forrest's Tangled Memory

More than one hundred years after the battle at Fort Pillow, Nathan Bedford Forrest became a touchstone in the national debate over Confederate remembrance. He is still honored by his supporters, but others are disgusted by his slave trading, the butchery by his troops at Fort Pillow, and his leadership of the KKK. Forrest's twen-

---

[72] Greg Mertz, email to author, August 14, 2021.
[73] Ta-Nehisi Coates, "The Convenient Suspension of Disbelief," *Atlantic* (June 13, 2011), https://www.theatlantic.com/national/archive/2011/06/the-convenient-suspension-of-disbelief/240318/.

ty-first-century critics have more than enough evidence to prosecute the case against his public memory.

Forrest's memory is entangled in the whole issue of how we think about the past. Monuments reflect how we see ourselves at a point in time and how we want past events to be remembered. Some are simple (if huge), nonpolitical tributes, such as the Bunker Hill or Washington monuments. American towns often feature simple statues of a lone soldier sent to the Civil War, World War I, or some other distant conflict.

Specific groups, or even nations, erected monuments to support a theory. The Daughters of the Confederacy installed "Defeated Victory" at the Shiloh National Military Park in Tennessee in 1917 to espouse the Lost Cause view that a sure Confederate victory was stolen by the fatal wounding of commanding general Albert Sidney Johnson and the nighttime reinforcement of federal troops.

The Lost Cause ideology emerged immediately after the end of the Civil War and flourished in the first half of the twentieth century. In 1866, Edward Pollock published *The Lost Cause: A New Southern History of the War of the Confederates*. He said the war was not fought over slavery; it was a battle to retain Southern values. In 1968, a professor of Southern history at Case Western Reserve University in Cleveland, Ohio, named Bertram Wyatt-Brown told my class he would flunk anyone who wrote that slavery was the cause of the Civil War.

America's view of how we see ourselves has been changing since the Supreme Court outlawed school segregation in 1954, triggering the civil rights movement. The issue of Confederate monuments exploded into public consciousness after the 2015 murder of nine African Americans during Bible study at the Emanuel African Methodist Episcopal Church in Charleston, South Carolina. The shooter had been known to proudly display the Confederate battle flag, which became a symbol of racism to many. Display of the flag was no longer acceptable.

Southern states begrudgingly gave up Confederate battle emblems embedded in their state flags. Public monuments to Confederate leaders came down. That would have been fine with

Robert E. Lee, who never wanted monuments constructed in his name. He joined the rebel army because of his loyalty to Virginia, not because of slavery or secession. Still, he was the poster boy for the Lost Cause, and he was one of three Confederates enshrined in Stone Mountain, Georgia, a post–Civil War Confederate version of Mount Rushmore.

In Lexington, Virginia, the home where Thomas Jackson lived while teaching at Virginia Military Institute is no longer called the Stonewall Jackson House. Now it's just the Jackson House. A few blocks away, Jackson's statue at VMI was removed in December 2020, while the statue of graduate George C. Marshall (of the Marshall Plan) has been lifted into a place of prominence. "It is an understatement to say the relocation of the (Jackson) statue has evoked strong opinions on both sides of the issue," said VMI interim superintendent Major General Cedric T. Wins. "VMI does not define itself by this statue and that is why this move is appropriate." VMI is paying more than $200,000 to relocate the statue to New Market, Virginia, the site of a Civil War battle where VMI cadets participated. In nearby Staunton, Virginia, the Stonewall Jackson Hotel is now the Hotel 24 South after a small protest.

Virginia operates a Museum of the Civil War at New Market that objectively describes key battles while displaying flags from the North and South. A film provides a sentimental view of the battle from the Confederate side. Increasingly, state and local authorities will have to ask, "Is this respectful to all the soldiers who fought? Is it unfair or offensive to anyone? Does it tell the whole story?" The state-operated museum in New Market doesn't pass the test. The sacrifices of combatants and civilians on both sides need to be fairly and fully told in public museums.

The line between right and wrong is controversial. A few people wanted virtually all memory erased. Some in Chicago questioned statues of Abraham Lincoln, who did not oppose slavery in Southern states when elected. In 2021, Boston removed a replica statue of Abraham Lincoln emancipating a slave, because the slave was kneeling. Critics also targeted a bas relief across from the Massachusetts

State House that depicted Robert Gould Shaw, a mounted White officer, leading marching African American soldiers in the Fifty-Fourth Massachusetts Regiment. The sculpture had been commissioned by the state to honor Shaw. Sculptor Augustus Saint-Gaudens included the marching soldiers, an element that dramatically enhanced the emotional effect and power of the work. But still it was a White man towering above African Americans. The monument was vandalized four times, most seriously during George Floyd protests in 2020, with phrases such as "Black Lives Matter."

Perhaps a Black soldier in the Fifty-Fourth such as Stephen Swails should have been the featured figure in the statue. He was the first African American to become a commissioned line officer.[74] If the statue were commissioned today, no doubt that would be the case.

Even seemingly apolitical Confederate memorials in national military parks have not been immune. In May 2021, I was walking the Shiloh battlefield with Greg Mertz. We paused at a Mississippi monument erected in 2015. "I'm not sure this would be allowed today," he said. It depicted two soldiers reaching for the unit's flag after the color-bearer was wounded. The color-bearer is not carrying a Confederate battle flag; rather, it's a flag unique to units under Major General William Hardee. The sculptor said his only goal was to honor soldiers in the battle. His previous work was the African American monument at Vicksburg National Military Park.

The Southern Poverty Law Center reported that 114 Confederate symbols were removed in 2015 after the Charleston church attack, but 1,747 were still in place in early 2019.[75] Surviving monuments included more than 300 in Georgia, Virginia, and North Carolina. There were nine observed Confederate holidays in five states. In 2020, at least another 160 Confederate symbols were removed.

---

[74] Len Riedel, review of *Stephen A. Swails: Black Freedom Fighter in the Civil War and Reconstruction*, by Gordon C. Rhea, August 29, 2021, https://blueandgrayeducation.org/2021/08/book-review-stephen-a-swails-black-freedom-fighter-in-the-civil-war-and-reconstruction/.

[75] "Whose Heritage? Public Symbols of the Confederacy," Southern Poverty Law Center, February 1, 2019, https://www.splcenter.org/20190201/whose-heritage-public-symbols-confederacy#findings.

In some cases, change is being driven by financial issues. One example is Stone Mountain, a state-owned monument on land previously used for Ku Klux Klan rallies. Attendance dropped after the South Carolina church murders, triggering a decision by the park's only hotel to pull out. The search for a replacement was difficult. Stone Mountain Park CEO Bill Stephen said, "All interested potential vendor/partner replacements indicate they will NOT bid on the RFP [request for proposals] without the State of Georgia dealing with issues revolving around the Confederacy." In May 2021, the park announced a few changes, such as moving Confederate battle flags to a less-conspicuous location and establishing a museum that tells the monument's story, "warts and all."[76]

Forrest isn't one of the Confederate leaders depicted on Stone Mountain, but he is at the center of protests over Confederate memorials. In 2020, Conner Towne O'Neil wrote in *Time* magazine, "There's a statue of him overlooking a cemetery in Rome, Georgia and a bust surveying the Tennessee State Capitol. A county in Mississippi, a city in Arkansas and a state park in Tennessee all bear his name, along with many streets and schools and buildings. There are more monuments to Forrest in his home state of Tennessee than all three of the state's presidents—Andrew Jackson, Andrew Johnson and James Polk—combined."[77]

O'Neil wrote a book called *Down Along with That Devil's Bones* about the efforts to remove, and retain, the legacy of Forrest. Students battled to rename Forrest Hall at Middle Tennessee State University, where a third of the students are not White. Activists on both sides fought over a Forrest statue in Selma, Alabama.

Tennessee even passed a law called the Heritage Protection Act as a layer of change-delaying bureaucracy after Memphis voted to

---

[76] Thomas LaPorsche and Joe Henke, "Changes Coming to Stone Mountain Park in Effort to Tell Complete Story 'Warts and All,'" May 24, 2021, https://www.11alive.com/article/news/local/stone-mountain/stone-mountain-meet-to-discuss-proposals/85-ce3ff537-7a81-427e-a16b-62bb8e4bf99a.

[77] Connor Towne O'Neill, "The Fight Over Monuments of Confederate General Nathan Bedford Forrest Holds a Lesson about Whiteness in America," *Time* (July 13, 2020), https://time.com/5865573/nathan-bedford-forrest-statues/.

rename Forrest Park. In 2017, the city of Memphis made an end run around the law by selling two parks (including the renamed park) with statues of Forrest and Confederate president Jefferson Davis to a nonprofit group, which then removed the statues.

Even more controversial was Forrest's grave at Forrest Park. In 2021, the Sons of Confederate Veterans moved the remains to the National Confederate Museum in Columbia, Tennessee. Also in 2021, the bust of Forrest in the Tennessee State Capitol was removed.

Northerners also have not owned up to their region's complicity in enabling and dramatically expanding slavery in the South. Abolitionists took aim at people like Forrest but didn't go hard enough at the bankers, shippers, speculators, and textile mill owners who also made fortunes from slavery. In 1800, a slave trader named John Brown stood up in Congress to defend the right of American merchants to engage in the slave trade. He and two brothers signed the charter providing land and a building for the relocation of the College of Rhode Island to Providence in 1770. It was later renamed Brown University. Georgetown University sold several slaves to raise money. Harvard Law School adopted (and later dropped) the family crest of a slave trader who had contributed land and money. Yale is named for a slave trader. The list is almost endless. It seems odd that it's only in recent years that these institutions have made any attempt to confront their pasts.

The economic issues go even deeper. Cheap, abundant cotton, enabled by slave labor, triggered an explosion of textile manufacturing in Massachusetts, Rhode Island, and elsewhere in the North. "The inflation-adjusted price of cotton delivered to US and British textile mills dropped by 60 percent between 1790 and 1860," wrote Edward E. Baptist in *The Half Has Never Been Told*. Four new mills in Lowell, Massachusetts, were consuming close to fifteen million pounds of cotton per year by the 1830s. New York City's commerce was so tied to cotton trading that its mayor, Fernando Wood, proposed in 1861 that the city should also secede from the Union.

Failure to confront our past, or to study it honestly, is human nature. Maybe Northerners have made slightly more effort at candor than have the present-day supporters of Nathan Bedford Forrest. Forrest's defenders say it is unfair to judge him by today's standards. Tennessee House Speaker Cameron Sexton, who voted against removing Forrest's bust from the State Capitol, said, "Trying to judge past generations' actions based on today's values and the evolution of societies is not an exercise I am willing to do, because I think it is counterproductive. It is much more productive to learn from our past and not repeat the imperfections of the past."[78]

One false legend is that Blacks fought for the Confederacy as soldiers. Historian Kevin Levin dissects the issue in *Searching for Black Confederates: The Civil War's Most Persistent Myth*. Tens of thousands of slaves were used as teamsters, cooks, and musicians in the Confederate Army. Some were brought from home as servants to officers. "But critically, none of these roles included service on the battlefield as enlisted soldiers." A small number did bear arms at times.

Forrest took forty-seven slaves into the Army and was paid for their services by the Confederate government, according to Levin, who has researched Confederate slave payrolls in the National Archives. A slave named Wright Whitlow wrote in a state of Tennessee pension application that he was a horse attendant for Forrest during the attack at Fort Pillow.[79] Referring to his Army slaves in 1868, Forrest said, "Those boys stayed with me, drove my teams, and better confederates did not live." He promised them freedom if they came with him.

African American enlisted soldiers carrying Army-issued guns did play a significant role in the outcome of the Civil War—as free men fighting for the North. Cornell Professor Baptist wrote, "Eventually the Union Army began to welcome formerly enslaved men into its ranks, turning refugee camps into recruiting stations—and those African-American soldiers would make the difference between victory and defeat for the North, which by late 1863 was exhausted and uncertain."

---

[78] Cameron Sexton, Twitter, July 22, 2021.
[79] Gene C. Armistead, *Horses and Mules in the Civil War: A Complete History* (Jefferson, North Carolina: McFarland, 2013), 44.

The quality of the Black soldiers was attested to by Daniel Van Horn, one of their officers at Fort Pillow: "Never did men fight better, and when the odds against us are considered it is truly miraculous that we should have held the fort an hour. To the colored troops is due the successful holding out until 4 p.m. The men were constantly at their posts, and in fact through the whole engagement showed a valor not, under the circumstances, to have been expected from troops less than veterans, either white or black."

The African American Civil War Museum opened in Washington, DC, in 2004 "to tell the largely unknown story of the United States Colored Troops (USCT)." A Wall of Honor in a National Park Service site lists the names of the 209,145 UCST soldiers arranged by regiment on stainless steel plaques. In 2021, a Black man was appointed US secretary of defense.

But some Americans don't want to honor the contributions of freed Blacks. At a 2021 Memorial Day Service sponsored by the American Legion in Hudson, Ohio, the microphone of retired Army lieutenant colonel Barnard Kemter was intentionally muted by two organizers when he made these comments: "Memorial Day was first commemorated by an organized group of Black freed slaves less than a month after the Confederacy surrendered. The ceremony is believed to have included a parade of as many as 10,000 people, including 3,000 African-American schoolchildren singing the Union marching song, 'John Brown's Body.'"[80]

In 1971, Tennessee acquired 1,628 acres to establish a historic and recreational park at the Fort Pillow site and conducted archaeological excavations. An inner fort was reconstructed but built stronger than the original and not quite in the right location. Controversy followed about how the battle was interpreted in a small museum. Was there a massacre? There were complaints about a short slide show discussing the fort's history. It was no longer shown. Today a film is shown that acknowledges controversy over the treatment of prisoners. One sign in the museum lists the names of the dead by

---

[80] Neil Vigdor, "A Veteran Tried to Credit Black Americans on Memorial Day. His Mic Got Muted," *New York Times*, June 3, 2021.

unit. The list of Black soldiers so overwhelms the others that a point is strongly made.

The river side of the site has changed dramatically since the battle. The Mississippi River shifted more than one mile west. A small lake called Cold Creek Chute remained, but fifty acres of the bluff collapsed in 1908, pushing the water even farther from the fort. It's no longer possible to hike the ravines used by Confederate soldiers who headed off the retreating Union soldiers as they raced down the bluff.

A rigorous 2.5-mile loop leads from the museum to the battle site and back. A free trail map at the museum shows twenty-two numbered locations of interest, including Forrest's first command position, an original redoubt, and points of attack. If you approach the fort from the south, you walk past steep ravines used by the Confederates to safely approach the fort. Then you pass the general location of rifle pits abandoned too quickly by dismounted Union cavalry. Then you pass the site of cabins the soldiers were told to burn but didn't except for a handful. The remaining cabins provided cover for advancing Confederates. And finally, at the reconstructed Union fort, you see the deep trench Confederates entered during the truce. After the battle, dead Union soldiers were buried on the south side of the fort. They were later reinterred in a federal cemetery in Memphis, the same city where Forrest's remains were located until 2021.

CHAPTER 6

"Vinegar Joe" Stilwell and the Battle for Burma

The future of all Asia is at stake along with the tremendous effort which America has expended in that region.

—President Franklin D. Roosevelt

We have had a hard scrap in this bitched-up jungle.

—General Joseph W. Stilwell

One of the tourist sites in Chongqing, China, is the General Joseph W. Stilwell Museum, a tribute to the man who directed American military policy in China and Burma during World War II. The museum, located in Stilwell's wartime headquarters, is operated by the city government.

It seems odd to find a memorial to an American four-star general in China, particularly since there is no Stilwell memorial in the United States. The museum symbolizes China's changing view toward America's role in its bitter fight against a massive Japanese invasion that resulted in millions of deaths and massive dislocations of people. American pilots, foot soldiers, and support personnel died along with Chinese soldiers in battles whose memory was long repressed in China and long forgotten in the United States.

America had a convoluted relationship with China during its formative period of 1937 to 1949, when the Communists took power. One focal point of heated debates was a 1,072-mile military supply road through Burmese and Chinese mountains. The section of the road in southwestern China today features museums and statues of Stilwell and American soldiers standing shoulder to shoulder with their Chinese counterparts. The memorials are an anomaly given the current heated rhetoric between leaders of America and China.

The statues make sense after a detailed look at the Battle for Burma and the desire of Chinese survivors and their descendants to preserve the memories of the horrific losses.

Key players included Chiang Kai-shek (Jiang Jieshi), head of the Nationalist (Kuomintang or KMT) government in China; US president Franklin Delano Roosevelt (FDR); Mao Tse-tung (Mao Zedong), leader of the Chinese Communist Party (CCP); and George C. Marshall, chief of staff of the US Army; and Stilwell.

A bust of General Joseph Stilwell is shown at the Stilwell Museum in Chongqing, China. (Wikimedia Commons)

FDR had family ties to China, and he had a prescient vision about the important role China would play after the war. One of the curios in his presidential museum in Hyde Park, New York, is a blue-and-white glazed ceramic vase from the nineteenth century. The keepsake is one of the relics from a fortune earned in part by FDR's opium-smuggling maternal grandfather, Warren Delano Jr.

FDR liked to tell China stories and fancied himself something of a China expert based on his family's history there. Historian Joseph E. Persico wrote, "Roosevelt believed that the most populous nation on earth, with a culture stretching back more than 5,000 years, belonged among the other great powers, and that it could be a strong American ally. But his sentimental, romanticized vision of China led to the creation of semi-delusional policies toward that country—policies that, over the span of the war, cost much and gained little."[81]

American policy focused on FDR's belief that Chiang's Nationalist government could anchor a postwar Asia free of colonial empires. Complicating the situation was bitter sparring over military policy between Chiang and Stilwell. They couldn't even agree on the enemy. For Stilwell and the Americans, it was Japan. For Chiang, it was the Chinese Communists. "Communism is a disease of the heart; the Japanese are but a disease of the skin,"[82] Chiang famously said. Chiang Kai-shek was yin to Joseph Stilwell's yang. Chiang, at war since 1937, was cautious and vacillating; Stilwell was aggressive and determined. Chiang would say Stilwell was reckless with Chinese troops. Their ability to work together to fuse Chinese and American resources and goals would be critical. It is still debated whose approach was most appropriate.

Chiang was a career soldier who assumed control of China in the 1920s and led armies north against provincial warlords and the CCP to consolidate his power. He was an anti-imperial revolutionary who had an old-fashioned conception of China's best interests at

---

[81] Joseph Persico, "FDR's China Syndrome," HistoryNet.com, https://www.historynet.com/fdrs-china-syndrome.htm.

[82] "Mao's Rise to Power," Sutori.com, https://www.sutori.com/en/item/chiang-kai-shek-communism-is-a-disease-of-the-heart-the-japanese-are-but-a-dis.

heart. He was a reactionary dictator who was brutal in his repression of dissent. Joseph Stilwell was a highly regarded West Point graduate who was called "Vinegar Joe" because of an acerbic personality that would become a problem with Chiang and British officers, whom he privately derided with slurs. He served from 1935 to 1939 as military attaché at the US legation in Peking (Beijing) and was fluent in Chinese. He was an excellent tactician who was also skilled at training soldiers. He was extremely poor at working well in a complex command structure in an even more complex country. The cultural gap was badly underestimated by both sides.

The Chinese Communist Party was founded in 1921 by Peking intellectuals inspired by the overthrow of the tsarist government in Russia. The CCP was energized by resentment over nineteenth-century foreign exploitation of China and Japanese aggression. Mao, a young leader in the mountainous Hunan Province southwest of Shanghai, rallied rural support for the CCP with land reform programs. Chiang's troops pushed Mao and his supporters to northwestern China in 1934 in a punishing six-thousand-mile year-long trek remembered as the Long March.

With one eye on the CCP and another on the Japanese, the Chiang-led Chinese Nationalists beefed up their military, starting with German advisers. In 1937, Chiang hired a former American Air Corps officer named Claire Chennault to improve the Chinese Air Force and organize a squadron of foreign mercenary pilots.

Japan invaded China in 1937 in what is now widely considered as the start of World War II. Chiang mounted a defense at Shanghai with two hundred thousand troops. The Soviet Union, wary of Japan itself, provided Chiang with military aircraft, ammunition, and funds. Chiang failed to stop the Japanese, eventually moving the Nationalist government 860 miles to the west to Chungking (Chongqing) from Nanking (Nanjing), which soon faced a brutal attack, remembered as the Rape of Nanking. The Japanese occupied much of northern China, the coastline, and major river ports. Chinese resistance hardened, frustrating the Japanese, who were anxious for a knockout blow.[83] Chiang took a defensive posture and felt his best strategy was a war of attrition. The Sino-Japanese War would last eight years.

In late 1938, the United States extended a $25 million trade credit to the Nationalist government, allowing it to purchase trucks and other supplies. More aid followed in 1940, and in 1941, when FDR implemented Lend-Lease, a way to supply equipment to Britain, China, and later, the Soviet Union.

Getting supplies to Chiang's armies became a problem as the Japanese advanced. Chiang dispatched two hundred thousand conscripted workers to build a 307-mile stretch of road in Yunnan Province through mountains to the Burmese border, where it linked with a road running to a railhead in Lashio, Burma (Myanmar).[84] The "Burma Road" was completed in December 1938.

The battle for China raged on. Chiang's forces won a battle at Taierzhuang, but the Japanese Army continued to roll and launched intense air assaults on Chungking in 1938. In the north of China, Mao's People's Liberation Army (PLA) fought a guerilla-type war against the Japanese that led to domination of large areas. The PLA more than quadrupled in size from 1937 to 1944. One major set-piece battle launched by the Chinese Communists was the Hundred Regiments Offensive in August 1940. Chinese armies directed by Chiang and Mao held down 400,000 to 850,000 Japanese troops. Leaders in Tokyo, anxious for more territory and raw materials, eyed an expansion of the war, with targets including French Indochina and Singapore.

Claire Chennault secretly promoted a plan in late 1940 to use American long-range bombers to attack Japan from China. George Marshall squashed the plan in part because no bombers were available. He said that one hundred P-40 fighters could be diverted from Britain to China. Chennault recruited one hundred Americans to fly

---

[83] Edward J. Drea and Hans van de Ven, "An Overview of Major Military Campaigns During the Sino-Japanese War, 1937–1945," in *The Battle for China* (Stanford, California: Stanford University Press, 2011), 32.

[84] Frank Outram and G. E. Fane, "Burma Road, Back Door to China," *National Geographic* (November 1940), 629–658.

the planes, forming a group that became known as the Flying Tigers. They were paid with American funds through a Chinese front called the Central Aircraft Manufacturing Corp.

Growing American support for China, coupled with a de facto oil embargo, helped trigger Japan's surprise attack against Pearl Harbor on December 7, 1941. Japanese armies rapidly moved toward other targets, including Rangoon (Yangon), Burma (Myanmar), and the supply route to the Nationalist forces. Japanese commanders also saw northern Burma as an important staging area for invading India and Yunnan Province in southern China, according to Japanese historian Asano Toyomi.[85]

The Japanese were aided by Burmese, who wanted to oust Britain, their colonial ruler. The rapid Japanese success created immediate problems, but the Allies' first priority was defeat of the Nazis in Europe. FDR hoped Chinese forces could continue to tie up the Japanese and that American planes could bomb Japan from Chinese bases.

On January 14, 1942, Stilwell was told to go to the home of Secretary of War Henry L. Stimson for a 9:00 p.m. meeting. They talked about China. Stilwell wrote in his diary, "[Stimson] has been looking all over for the right man to go out and run the show. Thinks the Chinese will accept an American commander. Told him I doubted it." Stilwell said he'd go where he was needed.

Command Confusion in China

Stilwell got the job and headed to China in February with the ambition of directing Chiang's army, but with no clear mandate except to help Chiang, supervise Lend-Lease in China, manage the Burma Road, and direct American military interests in what the Army now called the China-Burma-India (CBI) Theater. Chiang named Stilwell his chief of Allied staff with hopes of controlling the no-nonsense veteran commander. Acceptance of Stilwell was a neces-

---

[85] Asano Toyomi, "Japanese Operations in Yunnan and North Burma," in *The Battle for China* (Stanford, California: Stanford University Press, 2011), 362.

sary condition to get American money to pay for equipment and the often-crooked commanders of his troops. Chiang's inner circle and some Americans also profited from aid money.

One of America's top generals, aching for a combat assignment, walked right into a hot mess. "China was a place rather than a nation: a makeshift affair whose economy was wrecked," wrote Brigadier General Frank Dorn, Stilwell's chief of staff. "Tens of millions of its people had died from bullet, disease or starvation… It had become a police state whose authority—such as it was—depended on fear of the dreaded secret police." The CCP operated in northern China as a self-controlling state. Regional leaders akin to warlords controlled much of the Chinese Army. The Japanese occupied large areas of the country, brutalized the population, gutted buildings for metal scrap, and sucked out raw materials. Stilwell had three layers of command: the US joint chiefs (the only one he cared about), Chiang, and the British, who ruled India and Burma.

When Stilwell met with Chiang in March, the British were already withdrawing from Rangoon and planning a defensive line in central Burma. Stilwell asked Chiang for command of the Chinese Fifth and Sixth Armies in Burma. The theater commander was the newly arrived British general Harold Alexander. Chiang granted the request and also wanted Stilwell to have command of the British forces. Disaster soon followed. The well-organized, hard-charging Japanese easily defeated larger British and Chinese forces lacking cohesion and confidence. Japanese victory was "virtually assured" by the time Stilwell had arrived, according to Cambridge professor Hans van de Ven, writing in a 2017 book called *China at War: Triumph and Tragedy in the Emergence of the New China, 1937–1952*. Stilwell was blamed, however, for the loss of Chinese troops and assets because of his decision to mount a counteroffensive. "The responsibility for the enormous sacrifice of our forces in Burma lies entirely with Stilwell's command failures," Chiang wrote in his diary.

Stilwell walked out of Burma into India with an entourage of 117 in what became one of the more infamous retreats in American military history. Chiang's troops were left to fend for themselves. In

August, a story in *Time* magazine described Stilwell on his "heroic" march. "He did not look like a Napoleonic commander, performing a miracle of military endurance. He was only a plain, lanky, thin-lipped American, with a weather-beaten face, a dour smile, a sun-burned neck: he might have been a hunter in the backwoods of his native Florida. But like the plain, lanky Americans who hacked the nation out of the wilderness, 'Vinegar Joe' had created an epic—out of sweat and weariness and malaria, of retreat and desperation and endurance. And last week what he was doing for China was worth all the noble and encouraging talk in the world."[86] The article included this quote from a Stilwell press conference in India: "I claim we got a hell of a beating. We got run out of Burma and it is humiliating as hell. I think we ought to find out what caused it, go back and retake it." The *Time* article was an example of American media jingoism that elevated the Stilwell legend, often at the expense of Chiang.

A participant in the walkout, Captain Fred Eldridge, remembered it this way: "Uncle Joe [Stilwell], oldest man in the party, kept insulting everyone, telling the laggards they had no guts and getting each man mad enough to go on just to show the general they could do it if he could. It was only through this competitive spirit engendered by the general's sarcasm that we were able to make the trek. We all realize that now, but we didn't then."[87]

---

[86] "HEROES: Glimpse of an Epic," *Time* (August 10, 1942).
[87] "Eldridge Tells 'Inside' of Lusty CBI Roundup," *Los Angeles Times* (December 30, 1943).

Generalissimo and Madame Chiang Kai-shek with Lieutenant General Joseph W. Stilwell in 1942. (Photo by Captain Fred L. Eldridge/Department of Defense)

Stilwell returned to Chungking angry and determined to win. He told Chiang that his armed forces needed to be rebuilt from the ground up. Chiang, however, directly controlled only about one-tenth of the Army.[88] Stilwell had particular interest in reforming two groups: the nine thousand Chinese troops pushed out of Burma into India (designated the X-Force), and twenty-five divisions in the Yunnan Province, the location of the Chinese section of the Burma Road (designated the Y-Force by Stilwell).[89] The troops would be retrained, given new American equipment, and commanded by

---

[88] Michael Schaller, *The US Crusade in China, 1938–1945* (New York: Columbia University Press, 1979), 104.

[89] Barbara Tuchman, *Stilwell and the American Experience in China* (New York: Macmillan Publishers. 1971), 393.

Chinese officers under the guidance (and sometimes direction) of Americans. Stilwell established a training center in Ramgarh, India, for Chinese troops. At one time, Stilwell had also wanted to rearm and reform a projected thirty divisions in East China, a group that would have been called the Z-Force.

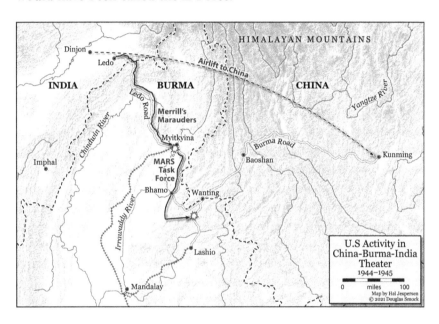

Americans played a critical role in supplying the Nationalist Chinese Army in its World War II fight against Japanese invaders. Supplies were flown over the Hump, while the Ledo Road was built through Burma. Two separate long-range penetration forces helped Chinese forces reopen the Burmese land routes. The map does not show Chennault's airfields in China.

The capture of Rangoon forced the Allies to ship war materiel to China by air transport from India. Planes had to fly over "the Hump," or Himalayas, which reached altitudes of nineteen thousand feet. Capabilities of the air transports were limited and were harassed by Japanese fighters after an airfield was established in northern Burma at Myitkyina (pronounced Mit-chi-nah; GIs called it Mishinaw; Stilwell called it "Mitch"). It took a ton of gasoline to move a ton of cargo to China over the Hump.

Construction of a supply road from Ledo, India, through northern Burma connecting to the Burma Road near the Chinese border became a priority. In Stilwell's strategic plan, the two reformed Chinese forces would attack the Japanese from both ends. Chiang preferred that Stilwell focus on boosting American aid to China but approved use of Chinese troops for a ground invasion of Burma. Creation of the Yunnan force was conditional by Chiang in part on the deployment of American combat forces in CBI.[90] The idea for the road did not originate with Stilwell. An India-to-China road had been formally proposed on January 1, 1942, by Chiang, who was concerned about the potential loss of Burma.

Around the same time, Chou En-lai (Zhou Enlai), a political officer of the CCP, contacted a Stilwell subordinate and indicated interest in working with the Americans. The Communists wanted American military aid. John P. Davies, political adviser to Stilwell, worried that strong support of Chiang could tilt the CCP more strongly toward the Soviets and result in a Communist-led China that would be anti–United States.

The Eighteenth Division of the Japanese Thirty-Third Army established headquarters in Myitkyina. The other major Japanese force in northern Burma, the Fifty-Sixth Division of the Thirty-Third Army, set up its base in Longling, China, astride the Burma Road in Yunnan Province. They faced the Chinese Expeditionary Force (the CEF or Y-Force) across the Salween River. Many were coal miners from Kyushu and dug deep fortifications. In their two-year occupation, the Japanese planted crops, built food processing plants, and housed "comfort women" in brothels.

Other Americans were soon at work in Burma. They were employed by America's new spy chief, a highly decorated veteran named William Donovan. In 1941, FDR had directed Donovan to establish a global intelligence network that became the Office of Strategic Services (OSS), the predecessor of the Central Intelligence

---

[90] Schaller, *The US Crusade*, 112.

Agency. Donovan shifted into high gear after the attack on Pearl Harbor, and Stilwell gave him the green light to create a guerilla operation that would gather intelligence and harass the Japanese at the Myitkyina airfield. Called Department 101, it was created in April 1941 and would play an important role in the Battle for Burma.

A debate emerged about the best way to prosecute the war in CBI and resupply Chiang's troops. Chennault wanted to attack the Japanese from air bases in China; Stilwell wanted Chennault's air force to support an invasion of Burma. Chennault also felt that the Chinese could be adequately resupplied by flights from India over the Hump. Stilwell argued for a new road. The British preferred an amphibious attack on Rangoon or other former colonies.

Army chief of staff Marshall told Stilwell to build a highway to link the Ledo railhead in northeastern India and the Mong-Yu road junction at the Burma Road, close to the Chinese border. Work began in December 1942. The route bypassed the heaviest concentration of Japanese troops, but much of the area was still under Japanese control. The work crew included fifteen thousand American soldiers, more than half of whom were African American. Eighty years after Blacks joined the United States military, they were still segregated and often assigned to menial or dangerous jobs, such as building roads, driving trucks, or handling munitions. Ultimately, fifty thousand Americans would work on the road with thirty thousand Chinese and Indian laborers.

Stilwell built the X-Force in India and refreshed the ranks with conscripts flown in from China. The returning soldiers had straggled into India after Stilwell's "walkout." Reorganization proceeded more slowly with the CEF. Soldiers for both armies were supplied by a major mobilization organized by the KMT's Youth Corps. The rallying cry of the eighty-six thousand who became soldiers was, "Link up Yunnan and Burma, fight with our allies, and exterminate the Japs."[91]

On October 4, 1942, Colonel Haydon L. Boatner was appointed chief of staff of the Chinese Army of India, whose headquarters was designated as Chih Hui Pu. Stilwell was commander, and Lieutenant

---

[91] Yunhi Zang, "Chinese Operations in Yunnan and Central Burma," *The Battle for China* (Stanford, California: Stanford University Press, 2011), 387.

General Lo Cho-Ying was vice commander. Boatner wrote, "Of course, the Chinese did not like to be under US officers—no nationality would! The fact that I, as Chief of staff, controlled all finances, supplies, even rations, gave me the leverage necessary." The first group of Chinese officers who resisted American leadership was replaced with more cooperative officers within four months. They had orders from Chiang "to play ball." The Chinese recruits were equipped with the Springfield rifle, caliber .30-06, Model 1903, a five-round, magazine-fed, bolt-action service repeating rifle. Both ends had to be shortened by contractors in India to fit smaller Chinese soldiers. The M1 semiautomatic rifle had become the standard US service rifle in 1936, but production was tapped out. Chinese soldiers were outfitted with a grab bag of uniforms made in India to Indian Army specifications. Boatner also recruited American officers to serve as trainers and liaisons.[92] The American military "adjuncts" played very important roles with the X- and Y-Forces. In April 1943, Stilwell opened a training center in Kunming, China, for the Y-Force.

There was limited combat in Burma in 1943 as the Chinese armies were rebuilt. One exception came from British and Indian troops, called Chindits, who, in a single mission in 1943, harassed Japanese communications and supply bases in Burma in guerilla fashion, taking heavy losses.

When Roosevelt and British prime minister Winston Churchill parlayed in Quebec in August 1943, Burma strategy was discussed. Churchill brought British general Orde Wingate to the meeting to discuss the Chindits' long-range operation behind Japanese lines. The US joint chiefs decided to provide a small force (three thousand) to be trained in India by Wingate. A call for volunteers went out to American veterans. FDR made it clear that US infantry would be limited to northern Burma and would not be used elsewhere in mainland Asia. Also in Quebec, the South East Asia Command (SEAC) was created with British naval officer Lord Louis Mountbatten in

---

[92] Boatner information comes from the 550-page "Boatner File" at the Marshall Foundation Library in Lexington, Virginia. Much of Boatner's commentary was handwritten on former orders and reports.

charge and Stilwell as his deputy. At the same time, it was becoming clear that China's role as an important front was slipping. The war against the Japanese would be fought through the Pacific. That was made very clear by June 15, 1944, after the capture of the Pacific island of Saipan, which was within bombing distance of Japan.

FDR still wanted a strong postwar China as an American ally and buffer against the Soviet Union. Keeping Japanese troops engaged was also important. FDR had invested significant political and financial capital in the worthiness of Chiang, who was reluctant to engage his troops against the Japanese while making substantial demands for matériel.

FDR's support for Chiang as China's leader may have wavered. At a meeting in Cairo in December 1943, Stilwell said he was told by Roosevelt, "We should look for some other man or group of men to carry on."

According to an account by Frank Dorn, Stilwell said he was ordered from "the very top" to prepare a plan to assassinate Chiang. He gave the job to Dorn, who devised a scheme to equip Chiang with a faulty parachute on a plane that would crash on the way to an inspection of troops. Dorn related details of the scheme, which was not implemented, in his book *Walkout, with Stilwell In China*. Dorn said he was also aware of Chinese plots to kill Chiang.

In the 2009 book *The Generalissimo*, author Jay Taylor detailed another planned, but never executed, assassination of Chiang. In the other discussion, Stilwell talked to Carl Eifler, who headed Department 101. Taylor implied that Stilwell unilaterally brought up the assassination plan after he heard that Chiang wanted his removal.

A large group of young graduates of China's army staff college was so angered with corruption in the military that they planned to seize Chiang when he returned from Cairo and force him to make changes. The plan was discovered, and Chiang ordered them executed or imprisoned. Throughout China there were widespread calls for democratic reforms that Chiang ignored.

To what extent the assassination palaver should be taken seriously is hard to say. A suggestion by FDR that Chiang should be replaced hardly mandated an assassination. It is possible that Stilwell's extreme angst with Chiang triggered frustrated conversations with top aides that he never meant to be taken seriously. His private diary makes no note of assassination discussions. No communications with Marshall or anyone else that I could find discussed Chiang's assassination.

Stilwell was not the only person who had his fill of Chiang. American diplomats in China such as William R. Langdon, American consul general in Kunming (headquarters for the Fourteenth Air Force), and Ambassador Clarence E. Gauss were increasingly frustrated. "There seems to be no real attempt on the part of the Kuomintang to solve the Communist problem; instead all signs point toward a Kuomintang hope that an American-equipped Chinese army can some day force a solution of this problem," Gauss wrote Secretary of State Cordell Hull on May 3, 1944.[93]

At any rate, Stilwell returned to China after the meeting with FDR with orders to finish the road to supply Chiang's armies in China. He went to Burma to take charge when command issues developed. He remained there almost continuously until the following July, leading in person his much-sought offensive against the Japanese.

The new American unit in Burma approved by the joint chiefs after the Quebec Conference was the 5,307th Composite Unit (Provisional). They came to be known as Merrill's Marauders after their newly named commander, Brigadier General Frank Merrill. He had a serious heart condition, and many of the Marauders were also unfit for duty. Code-named Galahad, the unit trained with the Chindits and was transferred to Stilwell. It was operating under a new group, called the Northern Combat Area Command (NCAC), led by Stilwell and with Boatner as chief of staff. The 5,307th Composite Unit would soon become a US Army case study in the disintegration of command.

Stilwell initially re-entered northern Burma with a force of about thirty thousand Chinese soldiers called the New First Army with a plan to advance through the Hukawng and Mogaung valleys

---

[93] "The Ambassador in China (Gauss) to the Secretary of State," *Foreign Relations of the United States: Diplomatic Papers 1944, China* 4, no. 2530, https://history.state.gov/historicaldocuments/frus1944v06/d575.

to Myitkyina in three phases. A British offensive would be launched farther south.

Journalist Theodore White wrote, "In December 1943 it could be truthfully said that never in history had Chinese troops launched a successful strategic offensive against a modern enemy. In the second Burma campaign, Stilwell proposed to rewrite history, staking his reputation on the unproven thesis that given proper equipment and training, Chinese soldiers were, man for man, as good as any in the world."

Stilwell's critics said he overestimated the Chinese. They also said he was a three-star general operating like a battalion commander. But Stilwell felt he had to directly lead recalcitrant Chinese commanders who had been instructed by Chiang to avoid harm.

For better or worse, Stilwell thought of himself as a foot soldier. Like General Ulysses Grant in the Civil War, he shunned fancy gear. He wore GI pants and a field shirt. Also like Grant, Stilwell was a general who would fight. And like Daniel Morgan at Cowpens, he talked with soldiers one-on-one or in small groups. He was often unrecognized, and more than one amazed GI asked how such an old man (sixty at that time) got into the Army.

Stilwell worked hard to build confidence in the Chinese under his command. In *Stilwell and the American Experience in China: 1911–1945*, Barbara Tuchman wrote, "He bullied, flattered and shamed, cajoled, bribed, goaded and pushed, rewarded with decorations, unit citations, press photos and every device of public relations, and kept the offensive going by the unrelieved pressure of his physical presence." Wounded soldiers received American medical care. Chinese fatality rates plunged; morale among soldiers rose. The Chinese would remember.

Stilwell went to India for a conference with the British, who commanded SEAC and had no respect for the Chinese infantry and had little interest in advancing China's cause. "The Limeys take me more seriously now. But they won't fight if they can help it." He said they "blew off" his head with "the plan," "global strategy," and "fancy charts, false figures, and dirty intentions," presumably a reference to their colonial interests, such as Singapore and Hong Kong.

In February, Merrill's Marauders moved out, starting on a new stretch of the Ledo Road. Three battalions were broken into six combat units identified by color. Existence of the Marauders was supposed to be secret. They even flew into India under the false cover of medical replacements. But security in CBI was like a sieve. "The night after we started our southeast march to the fighting zone, Tokyo Rose announced that American combat troops were for the first time marching down the Ledo Road," wrote Colonel Charles Hunter, second-in-command to Merrill.

Mules shipped from Texas, Tennessee, and Missouri each carried ninety-six pounds of saddle and two hundred pounds of equipment: light and heavy mortars, 75-mm pack artillery, heavy and light machine guns, ammunition, radio equipment, food, and medical supplies.

As the Marauders advanced, fourteen Japanese Americans working for the US Military Intelligence Service (MIS) helped to compensate for poor aerial reconnaissance. One was Sergeant Roy Matsumoto, assigned to Second Battalion blue combat team intelligence and reconnaissance, who had been recruited by the MIS for Asian duty while he was at a California detention camp. Matsumoto, who weighed 125 pounds, carried a 60-pound pack and a rifle weighing about 15 pounds on the long jungle marches. His parents had sent him to Japan for schooling, where he took compulsory military training. Incredibly, in addition to Japanese fluency, he was also familiar with Japanese military terminology. Penetrating behind Japanese lines, he noticed wires connected by poles. He climbed a tree, clipped a wire, and attached a phone receiver. He translated messages on a pad of paper, dropped pages to a soldier below with a radio set powered by a hand-crank generator. He knew the dialect of the Eighteenth Division soldiers from Fukuoka because he had delivered groceries to a family from Fukuoka in Los Angeles. A Lockheed P-38 Lightning was called in to bomb a nearby hidden ammunition dump identified by Matsumoto.[94] Both sides were using the same British maps.

---

[94] Roy H. Matsumoto, interview by Alice Ito and Tom Ikeda in Seattle, Washington, Densho Digital Archive, December 17–18, 2003, https://ddr.densho.org/media/ddr-densho-1000/ddr-densho-1000-153-transcript-b699ec23f4.htm.

While the Chinese made a frontal assault at a Japanese supply and communications base in the Hukawng Valley, Stilwell sent the Marauders around their flank, where they were bloodied. His intelligence officers intercepted a Japanese communication: "Cannot hold out much longer… No help available. Fight to the end."

One reason no help was available was a new Japanese initiative. On March 14, they launched an attack at Imphal, India, which, if successful, would have isolated Stilwell two hundred miles to the north and cut off airlift supplies. The Imphal assault drained British support, slowing his advance, as did early monsoon weather. Merrill, commanding the Marauders, had a heart attack and was replaced temporarily with Hunter. "We have had a hard scrap in this bitched-up jungle," Stilwell wrote in his diary in late March. He had a liver ailment but refused to leave the front. As Stilwell advanced with the Chinese troops, they found Japanese who had committed suicide by slashing their throats or by hanging in their dugouts. On April 11, he recorded that seventy corpses were found. Two days later, he wrote to his wife, "We are still plugging our way down the rathole." Conditions were horrible for everyone.

Stilwell ordered Land-Lease Army deliveries stopped because the Y-Force was not moving. On April 14, Chiang relented and the CEF (Y-Force) launched an attack in May across the Salween River with orders to take Tengchung (Tengchong), Lungling (Longling), Wanting (Wanding), and Namhkam in Burma prior to linking with Stilwell's X-Force. The CEF troop strength was 112,000, according to Brigadier General Frank Dorn, who headed the American staff. They were supported by sixty American fighter planes and forty heavy bombers operating from new airstrips in Yunnan. They were also supported by US Army doctors who cared for the wounded. The campaign is remembered in China today as the Battle of Western Yunnan and Northern Burma. Chiang wrote to Chinese commander Wei Lihuang: "The prestige of the Nationalist Army is at stake, as is the outcome of the war."[95]

---

[95] Zang, 386.

The Y-Force attacked four Japanese fortresses, suffering total casualties as high as 80 percent. At Songshan Mountain, 7,600 Chinese and 3,000 Japanese died. Assaults on the underground hilltop position failed until tunnels were dug, loaded with American dynamite, and then exploded. It was a tactic the American advisers might have remembered from the Siege of Petersburg during the Civil War. Seven American pilots died. A battle to capture the ancient walled city of Tengchong, astride the Burma Road, lasted 127 days, also with heavy losses. On October 5, Chiang ordered Wei Lihuang to capture Longling and Mangshi, which was accomplished in November.[96] Stilwell's pincer plan was underway. The dual campaigns frustrated Japanese efforts to reinforce beleaguered positions.

Working toward the Y-Force, Stilwell coordinated joint attacks between the reinforced X-Force and Merrill's Marauders as he pushed the worn-out and undermanned Japanese backward in northern Burma. Wingate's Chindits attacked targets to the south and cut Japanese supply lines to Myitkyina. Troops from multiple nations worked together under Stilwell on a moving front. Wingate died on March 24 when his plane crashed. The Chindits became exhausted and wanted to be evacuated. There was a presumption, if not a promise, of a three-month combat tour for the long-range penetrating forces. Stilwell refused. There was a war to win. Stilwell was also concerned that a large evacuation of British or American troops would undermine the morale of the Chinese, who did most of the fighting.

Stilwell used the Marauders as a spearhead to attack the airfield at Myitkyina in their third flanking sweep. It was a hundred-mile march over a mountain range. They moved out under radio silence in three columns that included 4,000 Chinese and 600 Kachin soldiers because their ranks were depleted from disease and heavy combat. Only 1,400 remained from the original 3,000.

The assault on the airfield was led by the Third Battalion of the Chinese 150th Regiment while the First Battalion and a combat team from Galahad were positioned nearby, according to a post-battle report filed by Major Fred Huffine, an American liaison offi-

---

[96] Ibid., 390.

cer with the Chinese troops assigned to supplement the weakened Marauders. Describing the action on May 17, he wrote, "Before any shots were fired, the 3rd Battalion crept up to the west side of the airfield. [American] fighter planes came in and buzzed the field. The Japs were completely unaware of our presence. Total surprise could not have been more perfect. The Japs fired small arms at the planes while the grinning Chinese noted the location of every Jap. Then the 3rd Battalion sent two companies crashing across the north end of the field. The Japs on the east ridge were astounded." One of the companies assaulted the Japanese positions, while the other provided mortar and machine gun cover. The Japanese withdrew, removing all but eight dead. Huffine continued, "Planes landed about an hour before the final assault [about 3:30 p.m.] and 12 gliders brought in Airborne Engineer equipment. All gliders crashed in, but the equipment was saved."[97]

Then the Chinese Eighty-Eighth Regiment was flown in, while the Japanese also rushed in large numbers of troops to defend the city of Myitkyina and retake the airfield. The battle at Myitkyina descended into chaos. Fresh-arriving Chinese troops killed other Chinese, mistaking them for the enemy. Stilwell flew in on May 18 with a dozen correspondents to take a premature victory lap.

In a later analysis, Colonel Scott McMichael wrote, "Inexplicably, in a display of gross military incompetence, Stilwell completely failed to take advantage of this coup-de-main. Instead of flying in strong infantry reinforcements, food, ammunition… Stilwell's staff deployed antiaircraft units and airfield construction troops! As a result, a magnificent opportunity was lost. Stilwell's mental lapse, which no one has ever satisfactorily explained, allowed the Japanese to build up the Myitkyina garrison."[98]

---

[97] "Operations of the 150th Chinese Regiment from 1 April 1944–4 August 1944," Boatner Papers, the George C. Marshall Foundation Library, Lexington, Virginia, 47.

[98] Scott R. McMichael, "Common Man, Uncommon Leadership: Col. Charles N. Hunter with Galahad in Burma," *Parameters: Journal of the US Army War College* 16, no. 2, 53.

There were other problems, including a rapidly rotating command structure of the Marauders because of illness and ineptitude. Adding to the craziness, on May 25 Hunter handed Stilwell a lengthy letter detailing complaints primarily about Boatner regarding the Marauders' treatment, prompting an investigation by the CBI inspector general (Colonel Stanley Griswold) that was authorized by Stilwell. Hunter also complained that NCAC intelligence, headed by Stilwell's son and namesake, had grossly underestimated the size of the Japanese force at Myitkyina. The suffering Marauders, like the Chindits, expected to be evacuated. Stilwell told them to buck up. Stilwell's direction of the Marauders was "erratic and nepotistical," the bitter Hunter later wrote.

A study of Japanese military records by historian Asano Toyomi showed that there were also command disputes and personality clashes on the Japanese side at Myitkyina.

The Japanese were also close to being broken. They received no ammunition replenishment, according to Colonel Husayaso Maruyama, commander of the 115th Infantry Regiment.[99] Their peak strength at Myitkyina during the siege was 4,500. Theodore White wrote, "The Japanese forces…decided to make a suicide stand of it, and each individual pocket had to be dug out in intensive fighting." Monsoon rains arrived, creating a quagmire. The Third Battalion of the Marauders was sandwiched by the Japanese. Stilwell told a field commander to send in engineers from the Ledo Road as emergency replacements. "This is one of those terrible worry days when you wish you were dead," he wrote in his diary. On May 30, he wrote, "[Twelve] men left in 2nd Battalion of Galahad [Marauders]. Galahad is just shot." The 209th Engineer Battalion suffered a 41 percent casualty rate.

One platoon of Galahad soldiers fought with the backs of their trousers cut out. Captain Fred O. Lyons said after the battle, "By now my dysentery was so violent I was draining blood… I was so sick I didn't care whether the Japs broke through or not; so sick I

---

[99] Interrogation of prisoner Colonel Husayaso Maruyama, Boatner Papers, the George C. Marshall Foundation Library, Lexington, Virginia, 236.

didn't worry any more about letting the colonel [Hunter] down. All I wanted was unconsciousness."[100] Chinese troops boiled water and cooked food and held up better. More than nine hundred fresh American soldiers, dubbed New Galahad, were rushed in and fought very poorly. They were also volunteer veterans.

On June 15, Stilwell wrote, "Bad news from Myitkyina. US troops shaky. Hard to believe." Some ran under fire. Some refused to obey orders. One angry and defeated GI publicly claimed he thought of killing Stilwell. A medic named Richard Murch reported on the high bar set for evacuation: "If a patient reported sick three days in a row and had a temperature over 102 degrees Fahrenheit for the entire three days, I evacuated him." In the book *Combat Veteran Stories of World War II*, Murch also said, "The Marauders were not always fairly treated by the Army's top brass. Weekend passes and leave were nonexistent, military awards were held back, and the atmosphere was, at times, more like a prison camp than a camp of a top infantry regiment. A common rumor was that the Marauders' awards could not exceed those of the Chinese army that reported to Stilwell."

On June 22, Stilwell heard indirectly that Mountbatten wanted him ousted from his SEAC command. Later, Mountbatten asked Stilwell to explain the Galahad "mutiny" at Myitkyina. The same day, Stilwell wrote to Marshall via encrypted radio transmission: "We have had to train the replacements right on the battlefield. Many of them could not use their weapons. There were some fifty psychopathic cases among them. Some of the officers ran away… Chinese units have all stood up to it in excellent style."[101] Marshall ordered an investigation into how such unfit, poorly trained American soldiers were sent to the front lines.

---

[100] "Merrill's Marauders in Burma by Capt. Fred O. Lyons," as told to Paul Wilder in 1945, http://cbi-theater.com/marauders/marauders.html.

[101] George C. Marshall, *The Papers of George Catlett Marshall*, eds. Larry I. Bland and Sharon Ritenour Stevens (Lexington, Virginia: The George C. Marshall Foundation, 1981). Electronic version based on "Aggressive and Determined Leadership," in *The Papers of George Catlett Marshall* 4, June 1, 1943–December 31, 1944 (Baltimore and London: The Johns Hopkins University Press, 1996), 490–491.

OSS operatives gave substantial support before and at Myitkyina. "The (Department 101) unit, consisting of 76 officers, 159 enlisted men, and 3,000 natives, supplied enemy intelligence, served as guides, cleared trails, and engaged in sabotage and ambushing," Donovan wrote to Marshall on June 19.[102]

In July, the Japanese were defeated by British forces at Imphal, a turning point in the Battle for Burma. "If it had not been for (Stilwell's campaign in northern Burma tying up Japanese troops), the Japs would have succeeded at Imphal," said British lieutenant colonel George Demetriadi.[103] An important role was also played by growing Allied air power. The Allies had taken control of the skies with more than four hundred fighters versus sixty for the Japanese.

Myitkyina fell on August 2 after seventy-eight days of grinding misery. Eight days later, the Merrill's Marauders were officially disbanded. It was strictly a paper transaction because the unit had already ceased to exist. Of the original 2,997 Marauders, only 130 were still fit for duty. Total losses at Myitkyina were 272 killed and 955 wounded for the Americans, and 972 killed and 3,184 wounded for the Chinese. Japanese major general Minakami Genzo had been ordered to defend Myitkyina to the last. He never left the battlefield, committing hara-kiri, ritual suicide by disembowelment, on August 1.

The role of the Chinese troops at Myitkyina was greatly underreported in published American media accounts and later books. Postbattle reports by American liaison officers such as Huffine showed that, with a few exceptions, the Chinese fought hard and were well led by commanders such as General Pon, who organized one hundred volunteers to attack Japanese positions inside Myitkyina on the last night of the battle. Boatner noted that the two Chinese regiments (88th and 150th) were heavily engaged in the combat, suffered a high casualty rate, and "evacuated very few men because of sickness or fatigue."

Air shipments over the Hump, now untroubled by Japanese fighters based in Myitkyina, doubled from June to late October.

---

[102] Ibid., 498–499.
[103] Tuchman, 530.

It was Stilwell's signature military victory. Many accounts blamed Stilwell for the collapse of Merrill's Marauders, but a 1975 analysis by the US Army Command and General Staff College detailed several reasons the blame should be pinned on Merrill and Hunter, the unit's top two officers.[104] It was never clear who authorized a three-month tour for the Marauders and Chindits. There was a lot of finger-pointing. The idea of a mass evacuation of American and British soldiers during fierce combat in a pivotal, breakthrough battle was absurd.

Stilwell was heartened by the victory of Myitkyina and prepared to continue the attack with the X-Force pressing toward the Burma Road near the Chinese border. In another broad flanking maneuver, fresh GIs would head south as a spearhead toward Bhamo and Lashio, the starting point of the Burma Road, and a railhead on the earlier route of supplies for Chiang's armies. The Burma Road from Lashio to Longling was paved and was a superhighway by Burmese standards. It was congested every night with Japanese trucks moving supplies north and evacuating wounded south. The Tenth Air Force kept the road quiet during daylight. The role of America's second group of mule-powered GIs would be to stop traffic and ease pressure on the converging Chinese troops.

---

[104] John B. Gaither, "Galahad Redux: An Assessment of the Disintegration of Merrill's Marauders," US Army Command and General Staff College, Fort Leavenworth, Kansas, June 6, 1975, https://apps.dtic.mil/sti/citations/ADB006689.

The Battle for the Burma Road

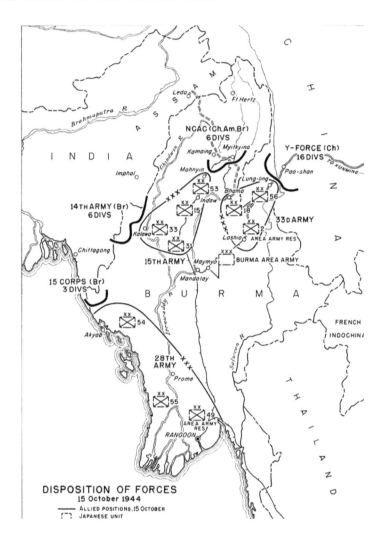

This Army map sets the scene before the battle for the Burma Road. Fresh US troops were training at Myitkyina as the Y-Force pressed the Japanese in southwestern China. The British were poised to press into southern Burma. (Source: US Army in World War II: The China-Burma-India Theater. Time Runs Out. Washington, DC, Office of the Chief of Military History, United States Army, 1959.)

Many books on Stilwell and China focus on politics and give short shrift to the northern Burmese military campaign. The first leg to Myitkyina may get some attention, but the next leg to the Burma Road is completely ignored. Burma was the forgotten theater of World War II, and Stilwell's second long-range penetration force fell into a far deeper oblivion. One reason is that Stilwell left Burma after Myitkyina for SEAC and CBI office work, which he hated. When he left, so did the correspondents. The phony romance of war propagated by some of the journalists had been obliterated in the blood-soaked and putrefied mud of northern Burmese jungles. For the new group, there were no newspaper-anointed sobriquets such as "Merrill's Marauders." There were no flowery descriptions of "heroic" marches. The secrecy of the next mission was maintained. The grueling slog and pitched battle ahead was unknown outside of long-forgotten military records, a Stilwell-sanctioned GI broadsheet published in India, and personal accounts, including recently discovered letters by my father, William Smock, a thirty-two-year-old buck private muleskinner on leave from the Associated Press office in Harrisburg, Pennsylvania.

Many of the second-wave American troops flew in on Douglas C-47 Skytrain transports during the battle for Myitkyina and saw the fight below. Unlike Merrill's Marauders, they were not combat veterans; they were mostly dismounted horse cavalrymen selected because of their training in animal husbandry and potential to care for the mules used to carry guns and supplies. They retrained at a new camp named in honor of the first Marauder who died in combat, Robert W. Landis, of Youngstown, Ohio. Also on their way to Camp Landis were three thousand Missouri mules, traveling by boat, train, and then walking the Ledo road with the 612th and 613th Field Artillery Battalions (Pack).

Lessons were learned from the collapse of Merrill's Marauders. First, the number of American soldiers in the second long-range force was doubled. Second, they received better training in jungle hygiene. Clothes were regularly rinsed in a DDT solution to kill typhus-infected mites. Physical conditioning was emphasized. Weaker soldiers were removed at Camp Landis. There was better veterinary care for the mules.

The role of the Kachin Rangers was better understood. The three most important officers in place at the Battle for the Burma Road were steady and effective. No undeliverable guarantees were made about how long they would be in the jungle. In fact, the GIs were told nothing. The Army did make a single promise: the government would send Western Union telegrams for the duration of the campaign twice a month to three addresses named by each man. Hopefully it would be good news.

Stilwell's new long-range penetrating force was activated July 26, 1944, but was not fully assembled until three months later. Officially called the US Army 5,332nd Brigade (Provisional), it was referred to as the Mars Task Force (MTF) and consisted of the 475th Infantry Regiment, which included the First Battalion made up of the remaining, mostly newer-duty Merrill's Marauders; the 124th Cavalry, a federalized Texas National Guard unit; and the Chinese First Separate Regiment. The 475th was bulked up with six hundred fresh graduates of the Cavalry Replacement Training Center at Fort Riley, Kansas. The purpose of the Army replacement centers was to bring regiments up to full strength. Many of the Cavalry Replacement Training Center trainees went to mechanized cavalry units, although 60 percent were trained as horse cavalry. On August 17, sixty-four Galahad officers with at least two years of foreign duty were ordered back to the United States. Their war was over. The enlisted men trudged on.[105]

One of the soldiers still on the march, and leading it as a scout, was twenty-two-year-old corporal Herman Manuel, a Puma Native American from Phoenix, Arizona. He was awarded the Distinguished Service Cross for helping evacuate "a wounded soldier under intense machine gun and rifle fire" in action near Myitkyina. Also on his second campaign was twenty-two-year-old corporal Wesley D. Kendle, a sheep farmer from Wyoming who was the mule leader in a rifle company. Another soldier was Private First Class William

---

[105] On September 15, the US military introduced a new system detailing demobilization requirements for enlisted men. Soldiers were sent home if they achieved 85 points, with 1 point awarded for each month of service, an additional point for each month of overseas service, 12 points for a dependent child under 18, and 5 points for a combat award or campaign participation star.

H. Unger, twenty-nine, from Danhill, Illinois, who had been one of the mercenaries in Chennault's Flying Tigers. He received a King's Commission in the Indian Army after the Tigers disbanded in 1942. "Bill said adieu to his first lieutenancy to become a GI" when he heard the US Army was forming the Mars Task Force, according to an article in *CBI Roundup*.[106]

The two mule-pack field artillery battalions each mustered about 460 men. Horses were originally included with the Merrill's Marauders, but they had perished. The Mars Task Force and other Allied forces operating in northern Burma had significant support from the recently formed Tenth Air Force: seven fighter squadrons, nine bombardment squadrons, four combat cargo squadrons, and three troop carrier squadrons.

Included in the Mars Task Force were twenty-four Japanese Americans working for the MIS. One of their leaders was Technical Sergeant Kazuo "Kaz" Komoto, a Guadalcanal veteran whose younger brother was in an internment camp in the Gila River Indian Reservation southeast of Phoenix. More than 112,000 Japanese Americans living on the West Coast had been deemed potential threats and were confined in camps. One of the jobs of the Japanese American soldier linguists was to eavesdrop on Japanese soldiers as they conversed around the defense perimeter. They also called out conflicting orders to confuse the Japanese. Burmese Kachin tribesmen as young as fourteen, operating through the OSS, acted as scouts. There were two portable surgical hospitals.

While Stilwell was fighting in northern Burma, the Japanese launched Operation Ichigo (Operation Number One) in China and quickly retook Chennault's forward air bases. It was Japan's largest land campaign of World War II, involving a half million soldiers, one hundred thousand horses, and fifteen thousand vehicles in the estimation of China scholar Hans van de Ven. "By October 1944, Sichuan was the only large Chinese province still in Nationalist hands," he wrote in *China at War*.

---

[106] Edgar Laytha, "MARS," https://www.cbi-theater.com/roundup/roundup 122844.htm.

American government support for Chiang had weakened. A State Department policy memorandum in May noted that the United States was "not committed to support the Nationalist Government in any and all circumstances."[107]

On July 22, the US Army Observation Group, often called the Dixie Mission, was sent to visit the Chinese Communists and assess their potential for military collaboration. They were impressed. Historian Barbara Tuchman wrote, "Mao Tse-tung was also thinking of American aid. He made it plain that he looked forward to American landings in China." She added, "The Chinese Communists of 1944 did not appear alarming, but on the contrary, like most challengers who have yet to succeed, rather attractive. In their rough and rumpled clothes, their earnest talk, their hard work and simple life, their energy, vitality and sincerity, they were a refreshing contrast to the world of the Kuomintang." Supporters of Chiang would have been irate at Tuchman's view of the Chinese Communists, whom they dismissed as two-faced opportunists anxious for military materiel. In January 1945, Mao Tse-tung and Chou En-lai asked if they could make their case directly in Washington, DC. American officials in Chungking sat on the request.

Alarmed by the rapid success of Ichigo, FDR promoted Stilwell to full general and pushed again to have him named commander of Chinese troops, including the Communists. His promotion recommendation stated that Stillwell "staged a campaign [northern Burma] that history will call brilliant." FDR warned Chiang that the future of Asia was at stake. Chiang initially agreed to make Stilwell commander of field armies actively fighting the Japanese in China and Burma, while Chinese Commander He Yingqin would retain control of a garrison army.[108]

The following secret message was sent via radio on August 31: "To General Stilwell for his eye only from General Marshall. When CKS (Chiang Kai-shek) puts into effect his agreement to place you

---

[107] Tuchman, 552.
[108] Peter Worthing, *General He Yingqin: The Rise and Fall of Nationalist China* (Cambridge, United Kingdom: Cambridge University Press, 2016), 226.

in command of all forces in China a number of changes in the India-Burma-China setup appear to be desirable."[109] Marshall said the Burma-India theater would be placed under a separate command. Lend-Lease deliveries to China would be determined by the joint chiefs. Lieutenant General Daniel Sultan would take command of the Allied force that would press the fight from Myitkyina to the Burma Road. Stilwell and Mountbatten would coordinate deployment of the Y-Force. The 1,600-word missive attempted to unjumble the ridiculous command structure that had been in place.

In September, two CCP officers told Stilwell they would accept his command. "Somehow we must get arms to the communists who will fight," Stilwell wrote in his diary.

Chiang changed his mind, calling FDR's demand a violation of China's sovereignty. Stilwell said he would urge total American withdrawal from China if he wasn't put in charge. In mid-October, FDR blinked and dismissed Stilwell during the last phase of an acrimonious re-election campaign against Republican Thomas E. Dewey. FDR tried to keep news of Stilwell's dismissal quiet before the election but allowed the *New York Times* to break the story October 31. He publicly dismissed the matter as a conflict of personalities.

Stilwell, who had accepted one of the most difficult assignments ever given to an American military commander, got no hero's welcome when he returned to the United States. Instead, a military policeman was posted outside his door, and he was kept under tight wraps. He was told to stay quiet until after the election. Stilwell privately received accolades from troops he had commanded, including the Chinese. One Chinese general wrote to him, "For at least three years you have made things possible out of impossibilities."

Stilwell was replaced with Albert Wedemeyer in China and Sultan in India-Burma. CBI no longer existed as an operational theater. The

---

[109] George C. Marshall, *The Papers of George Catlett Marshall*, eds. Larry I. Bland and Sharon Ritenour Stevens (Lexington, Virginia: The George C. Marshall Foundation, 1981). Electronic version based on "The Finest Soldier," in *The Papers of George Catlett Marshall* 5, January 1, 1945–January 7, 1947 (Baltimore and London: The Johns Hopkins University Press, 2003), 40–41.

Burma plan proceeded under Sultan, who was Stilwell's former deputy. The Y-Force continued to push the Japanese Fifty-Sixth Division down the Burma Road out of China. The Stilwell-trained X-Force pushed southeastward to connect to the CEF, just as Stilwell had planned. Ledo Road began carrying supplies to Myitkyina November 11. The X-Force confronted the Japanese Eighteenth Division with a numerical superiority of six-to-one, according to Japanese records.[110] The Chinese in Yunnan Province had a greater than ten-to-one advantage. Unknown to the Chinese, the Japanese had broken their code and knew what was coming. Estimates of troop strengths for both sides varied widely.

On October 31, Brigadier General John P. Willey was named commander of the Mars Task Force. He was a former cavalry instructor and had been chief of staff of the Myitkyina Task Force from June 1 to August 4. The 475th Regiment of the Mars Task Force marched out of Myitkyina November 15, led by the Second Battalion, and on December 16, the 124th Cavalry decamped. To Willey's frustration, the Chinese First Separate Division, which had been American trained and armed, was held in reserve by NCAC command. It was probably held back to replace Chinese divisions sent to Kunming in December 1944 at Wedemeyer's request. Chiang told Wedemeyer on November 27 that a decisive battle was anticipated at Kweiyang and that two of the Burma divisions might be needed.[111]

The Marsmen were outfitted with the Army's newly developed, fast-drying dark-green poplin fatigues and carried three to four days' supply of canned rations (mostly beans, meat, and vegetables) that were replenished by airdrop. Standard equipment included stubby machetes that were in constant use for bushwhacking and a dozen other chores. Many GIs carried their own hunting knives. Steel helmets doubled as cooking pots, washbasins, and stools. Later, when the men were trapped in foxholes, the helmets also became chamber pots. Most officers marched without insignia to avoid cherry-picking by snipers. Saluting was forbidden, for the same reason.

---

[110] Toyomi, 366–367.
[111] "First Meeting of General Wedemeyer and Generalissimo," Haydon Boatner Papers, Marshall Foundation Library, Accession Number 90, 125–126.

Members of the Mars Task Force on the way from Myitkyina to the Burma Road. (National Archives)

As movement south began, they passed roadbuilding teams working around-the-clock with bulldozers extending the Ledo Road at the pace of a little over a mile a day. At first, it was a wide, deep-graveled highway. Soon it was just a dirt path harassed by Japanese patrols. The Signal Corps followed the roadbuilders, erecting poles and copper wire for communications. Also at work were troops building pipelines to carry fuel to the Chinese armies and Chennault's aircraft. An estimated 1,100 Americans died building the Ledo road.

Kachin Rangers under the direction of Department 101 agent Jim Luce went forward to tell villagers, often scattered and afraid of both sides, that the Yanks were coming and were friendly. The Kachins scouted streams for the Americans.[112] As the 475th Regiment and the Chinese Thirty-Eighth Division approached Bhamo, another Department 101 agent (and Navy lieutenant commander), Pete Joost, had four thousand Kachin fighters armed and prepared to harass the rear of a Japanese garrison.[113] The 475th was diverted to Tonkwa, where it faced its first combat. The 124th Cavalry Regiment followed a slightly different route and also encountered sporadic Japanese resistance.

On December 10, William Smock, a drafted thirty-one-year-old father who went to horse cavalry school at Fort Riley, Kansas, wrote his brother: "I'm Number 2 gunner on a 60-mm mortar crew and wet nurse and confidante of the mule who carries our gun and ammunition… War in Burma resembles the French and Indian War (with new weapons) more than it does the war in Europe. The Boy Scout training in living in the woods is more value to me than any cavalry or open terrain training I had in the Army."[114]

Orders for the Mars Task Force changed January 3, 1945, when the CEF attacked the Japanese on the Burma Road at Wanting, China. Sultan ordered the Marsmen to hurry east to attack a rear Japanese staging area and a major ammunition dump on the Burma Road thirty miles south of Wanting at a village called Namhpakko.

The official history of the next phase, as seen by the officers, went like the following, in paraphrase: They faced two weeks of hard marching while cajoling heavily laden mules through narrow mountain paths at elevations as high as 4,600 feet. Several mules were lost when they slipped off rain-soaked red clay on steep trails. Heavy cloud cover halted airdrops for several days. Rations were short. Men got sick, were exhausted, and many were evacuated.

My father's first-person account, as written in a letter to my mother, was slightly different and captured the desperation of the moment. "Each day is the same. Up a damn mountain and then down one with, all of us so tired we could hardly put one leg ahead of the other. Every

---

[112] Richard Dunlop, *Behind Japanese Lines, with the OSS in Burma* (Chicago: Rand McNally, 1979), 342.
[113] Ibid., Joost, 331.
[114] William Smock, letter to Arthur Smock, December 10, 1944.

four days or so, planes were supposed to drop us food, but in Army style things would get screwed up and we'd miss connections. It was then I found out what it was like to go to bed with NOTHING in one's belly. Often streams would be far apart and we'd simply do without till we hit one. We were traveling east through Jap country, and no one could drop out or a Jap patrol would find him and torture him to death." Men with typhus or broken legs were tied onto spare mules, "but sick men, even with malaria and temperatures of 104, walked." Soldiers shot a water buffalo for food.[115] The standard for medical evacuation was even tougher than it was for the Marauders. There wasn't much choice. Only occasionally, a small propeller airplane could find a landing spot and remove one or two of the most-desperate cases.

When the 475th descended from the mountains at Mongwi, they were greeted by OSS agent Richard Dunlop and Kachin Rangers who had flown in after the battle at Bhamo. Kachin scouts had detected Japanese guarding the ammunition dump on the Burma Road seventy miles east. In between was another mountain range, called the Loilun, which peaked at ten thousand feet. The 475th and the 124th Cavalry were ordered to converge near Namhpakka. "Willey also tried, but unsuccessfully, to obtain the services of the First Chinese Separate Regiment," according to the official US Army account of the campaign titled *Time Runs Out in CBI*.[116] The attack proceeded with less than the strength Willey felt he needed.

After reaching a ridgeline on January 16, Colonel Ernest F. Easterbrook, commander of the 475th (Stilwell's son-in-law and former executive assistant), ordered a forced march to take the Japanese by surprise. They were approaching the Fourth Regiment of the Second Division on the Burma Road, where it ran through the Hosi Valley. Just north were the Japanese Fifty-Sixth Division and the 168th Infantry Regiment of the Forty-Ninth Division. North of them was the CEF. The remainder of the Japanese Thirty-Third

---

[115] William Smock, letter to Lois Smock, February 26, 1945.
[116] Charles Romanus, *The China-Burma-India Theater: Time Runs Out* (Washington, DC: Office of the Chief of Military History, United States Army, 1959), 329.

Army was south in Lashio and Rangoon. Namhpakka was seventy-seven miles north of Lashio. The goal was to block supplies and reinforcements from reaching the Japanese fighting the CEF.

As the Americans approached the Burma Road, they saw a rice-growing alluvial valley three miles long and one mile wide. On the other side of the valley were three hills rising to about nine hundred feet. At the south end was Loi-kang Ridge, which had an excellent sight line to the Burma Road, another 1.5 miles to the east. The town of Namhpakka, 2.8 miles to the north, could not be seen from the top of Loi-kang Ridge because of heavy jungle growth.

Easterbrook issued orders to take Loi-kang. The I Company of the Third Battalion was dispatched to block a road the Japanese could use for reinforcements and startled a Japanese unit en route, launching the battle. As American troops emerged from the jungle, the Japanese in the Fourth Regiment must have been stunned. The Americans had marched 279 miles over mountains up to ten thousand feet high in thirty-one days.

Major John H. Lattin of the Second Battalion of Easterbrook's 475th Regiment recalled the dash across the rice field and the assault on Loi-kang Ridge: "Passed through 1st Bn at 1400 and got orders to attack at once. Went down mountain and crossed a 2-mile wide rice paddy to next mountain, which is objective. G Co. in lead. About half way up all Hell broke loose. They were dug in and waiting."[117] The Second Battalion formed a perimeter and attempted to evacuate the wounded. Under the command of Lieutenant Colonel Benjamin F. (Frank) Thrailkill Jr., they dug in on the northern end of the Loi-kang Ridge.

My father's first-person account of the movement of the Second Battalion provided a muleskinner's view. He and other GIs moved into the rice paddy in a long file, expecting Japanese fire. "They, however, were taken by surprise." Darkness fell as the GIs began emerging from the rice paddy. "Once [it was] dark, the tired mules began foundering in the two streams and the swamp and we had a hell of a time. Several broke their legs or mired and had to be left. We were just up

---

[117] John Randolph, *Marsmen in Burma* (Houston, Texas: John Randolph Publisher, 1946), x. Lattin report.

the mountain [Loi-kang Ridge] a little way in pitch darkness when bullets started flying in all directions. To this day I don't know who was shooting at who, but tracers were streaking all around us. We just hit the ground and let the mules take their chances." My father's pack mule, nicknamed Sad Sack, had already been wounded five times. "In an hour the shooting stopped and we went halfway up the hill [and] we were told the lead company had been stopped by fierce Jap fire. So we stopped for the nite where we were. All was the maddest confusion—mules tearing every which way. Nobody knew where their squad was, let alone his platoon or company. I slept under my mule practically for lack of room. The nite was quiet, luckily."

He continued, "At 7:30 [the next morning], F Company was given the job of taking the mountain." A half hour later, F Company headed "up the mt side, me carrying 24 mortar shells, my rifle and some tommy gun ammo as well as my own and a mess of hand grenades. Man, I was heavy and EXPLOSIVE! I'll never forget that climb. Once on top we dug in and began plastering the Japs with mortar fire. By 3 p.m. they retreated back along the ridge like this:

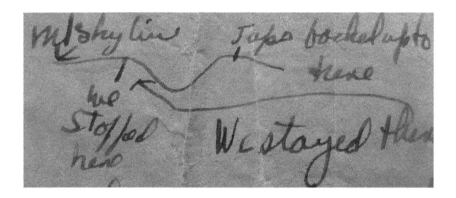

"We stayed there two weeks while we and the Japs made periodic attacks on each other. From the top of that we could see and shell the Burma Road—our mission."[118]

---

[118] William Smock, letter to Lois Smock, February 26, 1945.

The Second Battalion's prized position was also attacked by soldiers from the Yamakaze Detachment, who dug into a nearby hill with mortars and machine guns. Vince Trifletti, an American pilot evacuating wounded from the battle, described the scene over the Loi-kang Ridge: "When I flew over the ridge and dropped down, there were so many fires burning that the whole scene looked like it was being seen through a diaphanous curtain. The place was devastated. Every village, every basha (hut) was in flames, or was a smoldering pile of ash."[119]

Japanese truck and tankette are shown trapped by a crater blown in the Burma Road by a MARS demolition team. (National Archives)

---

[119] Dunlop, 378–379.

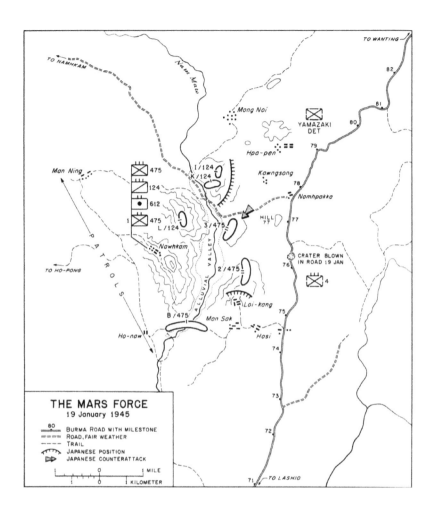

The battlefield was about four miles by four miles, with American forces concentrated on ridges about 1 to 1.5 miles west of the Burma Road, beyond machine gun range. Japanese were dug in on two of the same hills. American troops harassed traffic on the Burma Road with booby traps, bomb craters, artillery fire, and roadblocks of wrecked tankettes and vehicles. As Japanese infantry retreated south on trails east of the Burma Road, American patrols probed vantage points on that side of the road. (Source: US Army in World War II: The China-Burma-India Theater. Time Runs Out. Washington, DC, Office of the Chief of Military History, United States Army.)

Both sides soon traded artillery fire. Japanese 150-mm howitzers (range of 7.4 miles) massed fire on American troops in the valley, taking particular aim at a group trying to clear a landing strip. The US 612th Field Artillery soon returned fire and also aimed at approaching trucks on the Burma Road, using Kachin Rangers as scouts. John Randolph wrote in *Marsmen in Burma*: "The effectiveness of our artillery, coupled with close-in infantry action, was revealed by subsequent reports that some twenty truckloads of [Japanese] casualties were picked up for evacuation south" on January 18.

On January 20, events north of the fight dramatically ratcheted up the stakes. The Chinese took possession of Wanting, pushing the Fifty-Sixth back into Burma. Just west of Wanting, the X-Force coming from the opposite direction made contact with the CEF. The Ledo Road was now connected to the Burma Road in China.

Easterbrook asked permission to establish a position on a ridge just east of the Burma Road on January 21, according to *Time Runs Out in CBI*. The move would have established a much tighter block on the road. "Plan is good, but I have no report on Allied activities to the North," Willey radioed Easterbrook. He said after the war he was also concerned about lack of supplies. He surely also wanted to avoid the devastation of American troops that he witnessed at Myitkyina. It was a decision that would be criticized later.

After a large US Army air supply drop January 24, a rattled officer in the Japanese Fourth Regiment incorrectly warned the Fifty-Sixth Division that a large paratrooper landing was underway in the area where the MTF had dug in. Fearful of being trapped, the commander of the Fifty-Sixth requested permission to destroy supplies and retreat south along the Burma Road, right smack into the heated fight. The Rangoon garrison chief sent forty vehicles loaded with fuel north to aid in the panicky evacuation, which began January 25. First, the rescuers, moving north, had to get past the Mars Task Force, and then the evacuees, moving south, had to get past. It was a shooting gallery targeting Japanese traffic moving both ways. Bombers also pulverized the road but had little effect on pillboxes that dotted the hillsides.

The battle for the hills around the Burma Road rose to fever pitch.

Several Japanese soldiers charged banzai-style into machine gun fire or committed suicide by hand grenade to take out American positions. Japanese vehicles attempting passage, including small tanks, called tankettes, were blown up by booby traps. During the day, MTF patrols probed Japanese positions.

Burma Road traffic was largely stopped during the day, but vehicles covered by fire from the 150-mm howitzers slipped through at night. The chief of staff of the Japanese Thirty-Third Army personally directed diversionary attacks at night to reduce American artillery fire. There were also parallel trails east of the Burma Road where the retreating Japanese foot soldiers could retreat safely.

Meanwhile, elements of the Chinese 114th Regiment had been summoned to support the Americans and began to launch sporadic ground attacks on the Japanese positions four miles north of Namhpakka. The Third Battalion of the 475th took possession of a hilltop in support. A lone Chinese company established a block on the road and was almost completely destroyed by suicide charges by the desperate Fifty-Sixth Division.

Supply drops by C-47s were severely disrupted by Japanese antiaircraft fire. The only food for some GIs was canned fish and biscuits taken from dead Japanese soldiers. No quarter was given by either side. Army intelligence officers issued orders to bring in prisoners. Randolph reported that the 124th brought in two, one of whom survived for questioning.

The Japanese targeted observation posts used to direct artillery fire on the Burma Road. On February 1, a direct hit on the Second Battalion's observation trench on the Loi-kang Ridge killed Colonel Thrailkill and at least three enlisted soldiers.

F Troop, Second Squadron of the 124th Cavalry Regiment was ordered on February 2 to attack a Japanese-held ridge north of Loi-kang in a further effort to halt frantically escaping traffic on the Burma Road. All of the officers were killed or wounded. One of them, Lieutenant Jack L. Knight, commander of F Troop, was awarded the Congressional Medal of Honor.

His citation said, "After taking the troop's objective and while making preparations for a defense, he discovered a nest of Japanese pillboxes and foxholes to the right front. Preceding his men by at least ten feet, he immediately led an attack. Single-handedly, he knocked out two enemy pillboxes and killed the occupants of several foxholes. While attempting to knock out a third pillbox, he was struck and blinded by an enemy grenade. Although unable to see, he rallied his troops and continued forward in the assault on the remaining pillboxes. Before the task was completed, he fell mortally wounded."

In a separate action on February 2, Easterbrook ordered the removal of the Japanese artillery position on Loi-kang Ridge through a pincer action. Two companies of the First Battalion—Merrill's Marauders plus replacements—climbed the steep southern ridge, approaching the entrenched Japanese from the rear. Major Lattin, now the commanding officer of the Second Battalion, took a platoon from F Company and moved one knoll closer to the other end of the Japanese perimeter. There was heavy artillery fire on the ridgetop for fifteen minutes, and then the assault began. After several hours, the Japanese were compressed between the pincers, which were within eight hundred yards of each other. The Americans dug in, refreshed their ammunition, and called in carefully placed artillery fire on the remaining Japanese. In the morning, the two ends of the pincers joined using the code word *Chicago* for safe movement. The Japanese had abandoned the ridge overnight.

My father described it this way: "They got tired of being killed by snipers and artillery so F troop again, with help, attacked for keeps and really chased the Nips off the whole mt. They left for good and peace descended."

Battle for the Burma Road
Order of Battle

US Army 5,332nd Brigade (Provisional), Also Known as the Mars Task Force

8,600

Brigadier General John P. Willey, commanding

—475th Infantry, Long-Range Penetration Regiment, Special (included 1st Battalion of the 5307th Brigade, also known as Merrill's Marauders. Also included 600 dismounted troopers from the Cavalry Replacement Training Center at Fort Riley, Kansas) authorized strength: 3,049; actual strength on January 26, 1944: 2,513. Organized by battalions: Colonel Ernest F. Easterbrook

—124th Cavalry, Special (or dismounted) authorized strength: 2,073. Organized by squadrons: Colonel William L. Osborne

—Chinese 1st Separate Regiment (held in reserve): 2,600: Colonel Lin Kuan-hsiang

—612th Mule-Pack Field Artillery Battalion: 460 (75-mm pack howitzers)

—613th Mule-Pack Field Artillery Battalion: 460 (75-mm pack howitzers)

—Six quartermaster pack troops

—Six platoons Kachin Rangers

—44th and 49th Portable Surgical Hospitals

—7th Chinese Animal Pack Troop

Chinese 114th Regiment: Colonel Peng Ko-li

Imperial Japanese 33rd Army
(11,500 in the battle area)
Lieutenant General Honda Masaki, Commanding theater area from Rangoon garrison
56th Division: Lieutenant General Matsuyama Yūzō
4th Regiment, 2nd Division: Colonel Ichikari Yusaku
Yamazaki Detachment
168th Regiment of the 49th Division

Note: In March 1943, the Japanese umbrella command based in Singapore created the Burma Area Army (BAA), consisting of the Twenty-Eighth Army in southern Burma, the Fifteenth Army in Central Burma, and the Thirty-Third Army in northern Burma. Each had three divisions. Two reinforcement divisions were added to the BAA in May 1943. The Second Division, which was reconstituted in Japan from Guadalcanal survivors, arrived in early 1944. Total Japanese strength was 316,700, according to Japanese historian Asano Toyomi. The 168th Infantry Regiment of the Forty-Ninth Division and the Second Division were assigned to support the Fifty-Sixth Division in defense of the Burma Road following the Japanese defeat at Imphal, India, in July 1944.

An American soldier remembers a fallen comrade at a makeshift cemetery built near the Burma Road. (CBI Roundup)

The Mars Task Force won control of the Burma Road February 9 after the last remnants of the Fifty-Sixth Division escaped toward Lashio. Nine days later, Mountbatten visited the Marsmen and congratulated them for their work. The MTF lost 115 killed in action and 938 wounded. They buried 673 Japanese left on the field. The American dead were buried in three fenced-in cemeteries with rows of wooden crosses. Arrangements were made with local tribes for maintenance.

The MTF had fired 31,200 rounds of artillery shells into Japanese positions and onto the Burma Road. Close to four million rounds of all types of ammunition were fired by the American side. According to an estimate by John Randolph, that broke down to 322 every minute around the clock. He did not include bombs dropped by the Air Force.

An aerial US Signal Corps photo showed the Burma Road after it was reopened. (National Archives)

After the Ledo Road had connected to the Burma Road north of their position, supplies from India started moving to China. The first convoy via the newly opened Ledo-Burma Road, soon to be renamed the Stilwell Road by Chiang, reached Kunming in February 1945. The Mars Task Force did clear the Burma Road that extended south to Lashio, but the victory was, in a sense, Pyrrhic. The Ledo Road was now the supply route. It was not Pyrrhic considering the toll in men, matériel, and morale of the Japanese Army. The MTF attack also hastened the removal of Japanese from the area where the Ledo Road joined the Burma Road.

On January 25, George Marshall sent a radio message to Sultan: "Great credit is due to General Stilwell for his vision in conceiving the project of the Ledo Road and fighting grit in carrying it forward towards completion. The Combined Allied Forces have made possible what I think will be considered a great milestone in the history of the Far East."[120]

General Willey of the Mars Task Force was criticized for not establishing a full block on the Burma Road. The commander of the Thirty-Eighth Chinese Division operating farther south complained that failure to block the road allowed the Japanese to make a stronger attack on their position. For its part, the Japanese Army had used a suicide squad in January to block the Ledo Road Between Namhkam and Wanting.[121] Once they were cleared, convoys began moving.

---

[120] George C. Marshall, *The Papers of George Catlett Marshall*, eds. Larry I. Bland and Sharon Ritenour Stevens (Lexington, Virginia: The George C. Marshall Foundation, 1981). Electronic version based on "Aggressive and Determined Leadership," in *The Papers of George Catlett Marshall* 4, June 1, 1943–December 31, 1944 (Baltimore and London: The Johns Hopkins University Press, 1996), 563–566.

[121] "Convoy Reaches Jump Off Point," *CBI Roundup* 3, no. 19 (January 18, 1945), https://www.cbi-theater.com/roundup/roundup011845.html.

Trucks started moving on the Burma Road to Chiang's armies in China in January 1945. (National Archives)

Units of the MTF had marched, often with minimal rations, as far as three hundred miles and crossed four mountain ranges. At one point artillery and mules crossed the fast-moving Shweli River on a shaky bamboo bridge. After the battle for the Burma Road, the task force was flown north to train Chinese troops. My father flew into Kunming, was housed in a comfortable Air Force barracks, and longed to return home, but he was well short of the service points required for demobilization. He was assigned to *Stars and Stripes*, the Army newspaper, and was posted to Shanghai as news editor. Chiang ordered his troops home. Two thousand Missouri mules survived and were given to Chinese pack forces. On June 11, the Mars Task Force was disbanded. Major Reuben A. Holden told the Second Battalion, "It is not easy for us to see this outfit dissolved. The 475th Infantry made a spectacular record in Burma, one of which we can all be duly proud… I want each man in this battalion to know how sincerely I appreciate the cooperation and goodwill I have received since assuming command."[122] The battered survivors of the Japanese Burma Area Army surrendered August 15. Merrill's Marauders and the Mars Task Force were the only US infantry combat forces on the Asian mainland in World War II.

Most of America's ten thousand combat infantrymen in Asia in World War II were citizen soldiers. Private Harry L. Van Leuven of First Battalion, Merrill's Marauders, became an assembler for Ametek's US Gauge Division in Sellersville, Pennsylvania, for thirty-four years, retiring in 1985. One of the soldiers who particularly struggled on the long marches to the Burma Road was twenty-year-old corporal Jack Schweibold of Dayton, Ohio, who had lingering injuries from a childhood car accident and multiple surgeries. After the war, Schweibold taught English at Kent State University.[123] Donald J. West, who had trained in the horse cavalry at Fort Riley, Kansas, ran a medical supply business in Seattle, Washington, well into his eighties.[124]

The concept of a long-range penetration force in Burma originated with British general Orde Wingate, but it was significantly adapted by Stilwell. In Wingate's concept, troops operated in a hit-and-run, get-in-and-get-out approach. For Stilwell, long-range penetration was intended to take and hold ground as a supplement to, or spearhead for, larger infantry forces. He used his long-range forces in stealthy, fast-moving flanking maneuvers slightly reminiscent of Confederate general Stonewall Jackson during the Civil War. The tactic was punishing, but very effective. The Chindits flew in on gliders; Stilwell's soldiers marched with mules.

The long-range ground concept became obsolete as helicopters became the new cavalry. The mules used in Vietnam just a little more than twenty years later were M274 mechanized Mules introduced in 1956. The six hundred cavalrymen in the 475th Regiment of the Mars Task who trained at Fort Riley were the end of the line. The Horse Cavalry School closed in 1946.

---

[122] 2nd Battalion Headquarters Memorandum, June 30, 1945, William Smock records held by the Stratton family, Plainfield, Illinois.
[123] Conversation with the author, April 26, 1986.
[124] Conversation with the author, April 27, 1986.

The Ledo Road and the Burma Road are insignificant today. A writer named Donovan Webster tried to walk the old Ledo Road in India and was stopped after a few miles by armed guards. Sections of the old road still exist in China. The old Ledo Road in Myanmar (modern-day Burma) is covered with jungle growth and is only accessible with a permit and escort.

In June 1945 General Douglas MacArthur named Stilwell commander of the Tenth Army on Okinawa and prepared for an invasion that became moot when the atomic bomb was dropped on Hiroshima August 6. He died October 12, 1946, of liver cancer.

In late 1945, FDR's successor as president, Harry Truman, sent Marshall to China in an effort to seek reconciliation between the CCP and the Nationalists. He seemed to make headway, but talks fell apart in January 1947. Civil war resumed until the Chinese Communist Party won in 1949, pushing Chiang's government to Taiwan. One year later, Mao sent troops into Korea to fight Americans. Close to one million Chinese were killed or wounded, and the US Marines were forced into a debilitating withdrawal at the Chosin Reservoir, one of the few retreats in their history.

In 1951 MacArthur called the Marshall mission "one of the greatest blunders in American diplomatic history, for which the free world is now paying in blood and disaster." MacArthur had advocated invading China during the Korean War, with an assault force that included Chiang's army, which was on Taiwan, the new home for his government. Use of nuclear weapons against China was contemplated. Senator Joseph McCarthy blasted Marshall for making errors that he said allowed the CCP to gain strength. A debate on "Who Lost China" raged. One of the targets was Stilwell's political adviser, John P. Davies, whose loyalty was challenged.

In 1962, Mao—sensing his popularity slipping—rebooted his cult of personality and denounced Soviet premier Nikita Khrushchev as a phony Communist. He collected his quotations in a little red book and made it mandatory reading, first for soldiers, and then students. It spawned the fervor known as the Cultural Revolution of 1966 to 1976.

Facing a Soviet nuclear threat, Mao and Zhou agreed to detente with the US in 1972 despite strong internal opposition. By 2021 a reformed China was a major world power and on the verge of becoming the world's largest economy. Along the way, the nature of Chinese Communism evolved.

American and Chinese Memory

Is there any American memory of Burma, the Mars Task Force, or Stilwell?

Two somewhat-popular movies were made about WWII Burma. A 1945 fictional movie called *Objective, Burma!* starred Errol Flynn leading American paratroopers on a mission to capture a Japanese radar station. Winston Churchill slammed the movie for falsely Americanizing the war in Burma and it was banned in Britain. Despite the movie's absurd distortion of history, it was nominated for three Academy Awards, including Best Story. Churchill's criticism of *Objective, Burma!* was fair, but hypocritical. He had staunchly opposed the war in Burma. *Merrill's Marauders*, a movie based on a factual account, was released in 1962 and was moderately successful at the box office. The Stilwell character made cameo appearances in both movies. There were at least three other, even more forgettable movies about the war in Burma.

The exploits of the Mars Task Force are remembered in a very small exhibit in a modest museum in the old cavalry section at Fort Riley, Kansas. More interesting is the stone house where Brevet Major General George Armstrong Custer lived when he commanded horse cavalry after the Civil War.

In 1972, a monument was erected in Mineral Wells, Texas, to honor hometown hero Jack Knight, and Mountbatten attended the dedication ceremony. Knight's body was buried in Holders Memorial Chapel Cemetery in Cool, Texas. The Mars Task Force received a memorial stone at Fort Bragg, North Carolina, in 2012 and is recognized today as part of the lineage of the Seventy-Fifth Army Ranger Regiment. Many of Stilwell's Burma troops were inducted into the Rangers Hall of Fame, including Marauder Roy Matsumoto. No reason was ever stated why the

Task Force was called Mars (also designated as MARS). Like Department 101, it was apparently just an arbitrary name.

The Flying Tigers are remembered in the Guilin Flying Tigers Heritage Park in the Lingui District of Guilin. The museum is located in a cave that Chennault used as his command post.

In 2010, Congress awarded the Congressional Gold Medal to the six thousand Japanese Americans who served in the Military Intelligence Service in World War II. The Japanese American Memorial to Patriotism During World War II in Washington, DC, is a National Park Service site honoring veterans. It also notes the sacrifice made by those confined in camps. Major General Charles Willoughby, an intelligence officer for MacArthur, said, "The Nisei [Japanese Americans] shortened the Pacific War by two years and saved possibly a million American lives."

One important memory of the Mars Task Force is a book called *Marsmen in Burma*, written by John Randolph, who before World War II wrote advertisements for buses in Houston, Texas. In 1942, at age thirty-two, he volunteered to serve in the 124th Cavalry of the Texas National Guard. It was boring duty patrolling the border with Mexico, which was considered a threat early in the war. In 1944, the 124th Cavalry was sent to Fort Riley, Kansas, and soon shipped out to Burma. Randolph was a private first class who worked for the Army Public Relations Office (PRO), which asked him to keep a running account of what happened. Randolph witnessed the action at the Burma Road from the 124th headquarters bivouac, where he gathered many firsthand accounts, including officers' notes. The PRO decided his account was too long for its use and gave him the rights. In 1946, he self-published *Marsmen in Burma*, intending only that it be a keepsake for members of the Mars Task Force. Copies of the original edition now sell for $500 to $600 on various websites. His widow published a second edition after he died in 1972. The book was published again in 1990 with funding from the Missouri Muleskinners' Society. It was written from an enlisted man's perspective with an unusual candor, and even humor at times, including anecdotes of bartering with the locals for chicken and eggs or with Chinese soldiers for Japanese booty in a macabre postbattle flea market. The scuttlebutt was that Japanese swords in excellent condition, which were extremely difficult to get out of the jungle, could be resold to rear echelon officers (particularly Air Force) for $500 ($7,600 in 2021 dollars). One soldier who sent a Japanese major's samurai sword home was Technical Sergeant H. E. Newman of Gastonia, North Carolina, whose wife "was offered the entire (jewelry) store for the trophy's three larger stones," according to a story in *CBI Roundup*.[125]

The definitive accounts of Stilwell in the CBI and the military action in northern Burma were written by US Army historians Charles F. Romanus and Riley Sunderland, who had access to primary official source materials, and commanders such as Willey.

One of the other useful sources of information about the Burma campaign is, improbably, a military newspaper called *CBI Roundup*, the first overseas theater newspaper in World War II. Stilwell felt GIs needed a place to vent their frustrations much as he did, albeit privately, in his diary and command journal. Its first editor, Captain Fred Eldridge, on leave from the *Los Angeles Times*, said, "Uncle Joe will let us go after almost anything as long as we're sure of our facts. He figures the paper is a safety valve wherein the groaning GI soldier in the bush can get rid of his woes." In its second issue on September 24, 1942, Stilwell wrote, "It's your paper, so feel free to contribute to it. If you have a gripe, write a letter to the editor. If you can run the paper better than he can, tell him so, but watch out that he doesn't put you on the staff and make you prove it." Peak circulation was 120,000, mostly in India. Copies were airdropped to the penetration forces operating behind Japanese lines.[126] Soldiers in the field working for the PRO, such as John Randolph, contributed spot news. An amusing story published January 11, 1945, and written in Randolph's inimitable style, reported on the "capture" of Corporal Tokyo (Tony) Uemoto, Honolulu-born member of the Mars Task Force, by allied Chinese forces.[127] *CBI Roundup* can be read online.

---

[125] Laytha MARS profile, *CBI Roundup*.
[126] E. Gartley Jaco, "At Long Last, Roundup's Own Story," https://www.cbi-theater.com/roundup/roundup-story.html.
[127] "JapYank Becomes Japanese Prisoner," *CBI Roundup*, https://www.cbi-theater.com/roundup/roundup011145.html.

Another interesting source of information about CBI was Clare Booth Luce, wife of *Time-Life* publisher Henry Luce, who was tight with Madame Chiang Kai-shek. A report she wrote for *Life Magazine* described a meeting on April 7, 1942, between Stilwell, Chiang, Chiang's generals, and the British command in which they agreed to take the offensive in the First Burma campaign. After the meeting, Chinese troops moved to Mandalay to relieve British troops.

Scars from World War II still run very deep in China. There has never been a full accounting of war dead, but the number is at least 10 million soldiers and another 10 to 20 million civilians. That compares to some 400,000 for the United States. The Soviet Union suffered losses estimated at 20 million. There were more than 80 million Chinese refugees. The number of Japanese soldiers killed in the Sino-Japanese War was 410,000 with more than double that number listed as casualties.[128]

A Chinese poster celebrated the joining of the Burma and Ledo roads at Mung-Yu junction. (Wikimedia Commons)

---

[128] Drea, 46.

One memory of the war in Beijing is the Chinese People's Anti-Japanese War Memorial Hall. It includes a Hall of Japanese Military Atrocities. A museum in Nanjing commemorates the brutal slaughter that started in 1937. An English poet said that Nanking was China's Dachau.

Stilwell holds a powerful role in Chinese memory. His Chongqing museum opened in 1994 and was renovated with funds from four US groups: the Joseph W. Stilwell Institute Foundation, the Freeman Foundation, Stilwell Innovation Enterprises, and the Stilwell International Innovation Center. There are statues of Stilwell along the old Burma Road in China. He and his American soldiers are revered along with the Chinese soldiers who fought the Japanese.

Stilwell is respected in China today because he came to the aid of the Chinese people when they were being crushed and humiliated by the Japanese. Maybe there is no room in America's memory for Stilwell because of his support for military aid to the Chinese Communists. Or because of his abrasiveness. Or maybe he was just overshadowed by towering WWII military figures such as Dwight Eisenhower, Douglas MacArthur, and George Patton. Probably, he was forgotten because China was back-page news, his combat accomplishments were minimal, and his feud with Chiang induced headaches.

In the 2014 film called *Tracing the Steps of General Stilwell*, two of Stilwell's grandchildren explored key sites. They were greeted warmly by random Chinese as they visited memorials and museums along the Stilwell Road. They visited a restaurant and bar with pictures of Stilwell and some of the 6,500 Americans who served in the Yunnan Province.

At the entrance to the West Yunnan Anti-Japanese War Museum in Tengchong they saw a sculpture of their grandfather holding binoculars. A thousand helmets, some bullet-riddled, were mounted on a wall. At a nearby memorial, statues of Stilwell and Chennault had garlands of fresh flowers on their heads. On a hillside were 3,346 markers for each soldier killed in the battle to capture Tengchong in 1944. Most were unmarked because there were mass cremations of the dead. One cup of ashes was buried at each marker.

Their next stop was the monument to the Battle for Songshan. There were 402 concrete Terracotta-like statues honoring soldiers, including Stilwell and eighteen other Americans. The idea for the memorial, built in 2013, came from a local farmer and amateur historian named Yang Guogang.[129] Twenty-eight CEF veterans alive at the time of the monument's creation were depicted at their age at that time, including one woman. In another section, soldiers as young as thirteen were shown.

A monument built soon after the war at Songshan by Chiang's government was destroyed by Red Guards during the Cultural Revolution. The monument was reconstructed in 2004 and added to the list of monuments of the People's Republic of China in 2006. The new monument inspired by Terracotta Warriors was built in 2013.

Since the visit to Yunnan by Steven and Nya Stilwell, a new museum opened in Tengchong, the Stilwell Road Museum, featuring more than five thousand artifacts from a private Chinese collector, including Dodge trucks, Willys jeeps, and road construction tools. The Stilwell Road is described as a "lifeline for the War of Resistance Against Japanese Aggression".

There are tributes to Stilwell in Yunnan even though he was not present for the fighting there. He led the X-Force in northern Burma, and designated Dorn to lead the Y-Force American staff. On July 12, Stilwell briefly mentioned Dorn and Tengchung in his diary. It was far from top of mind as he struggled at Myitkyina and feuded with Mountbatten. In August and September, he was on office duty in Ceylon (Sri Lanka) for SEAC and India and China for CBI. Stilwell and Chiang argued about the Yunnan force in a meeting in Chungking September 15.

No matter. Stilwell is the American memorialized along the bloody campaign track of the CEF that was aided by Dorn's staff and the Army Air Force. Everyone seems to think Stilwell was actually in the fight. His statue at Songshan even depicted him in a Chinese uniform, which he never wore. He did sometimes wear a long-billed Chinese infantry hat. Stilwell has been mythologized by the Chinese in the past twenty or so years. To them, Stilwell symbolized a powerful American commitment, a great friend in a time of need.

---

[129] Rana Mitter, *China's Good War: How World War II Is Shaping a New Nationalism* (Cambridge, Massachusetts: Belknap Press, 2020), 4.

From 1937 to 1941, the Chinese had fought a Japanese Army of several hundred thousand with token support. Stilwell had no respect for Chiang, or many of his corrupt commanders, but he greatly admired the Chinese soldier.

Battles against the Japanese—Guadalcanal, Iwo Jima, and Midway—remain vivid to many Americans, while the names of the giant Chinese battles, such as Taierzhuang in 1938, are unknown. The Chinese do recall their huge sacrifices, victories, and losses. And they celebrate the role of Stilwell, the builders of the Ledo Road, and the small band of Americans who finally liberated the Burmese section of the Burma Road.

British China expert Rana Mitter wrote in 2020, "There is a strong relationship between China's memory of its experience of World War II and its present-day nationalist identity at home and global role abroad." That's a sentiment that has grown over the past thirty years, and has been building, he wrote in the book titled *China's Good War: How World War II Is Shaping a New Nationalism*. "China's engagement with other countries has become deeply shaped by ideas about the Second World War—both by the events and purpose of the war, and by its legacy. This is a major shift from how it previously presented itself."[130]

Streets in three American cities were named after Stilwell, but there are no statues or museums. His home in Carmel, California, is a private residence.

Stilwell's most important memory in the United States are his personal writings—diary entries, command journal, and letters—that were collected by his wife, Winifred, in a book published in 1948 called *The Stilwell Papers*. Stilwell recorded events bluntly in rough language. Chiang was the "Peanut," British were "Limeys," Mountbatten was "Glamor Boy," diplomats were "gasbags," and the Japanese were "little bastards." He respected tough guys like Stalin, whom he personally congratulated on the twenty-sixth anniversary of the formation of the Red Army.

Stilwell's writings were intended strictly for his personal use, but his widow felt he deserved to be heard. His recall had left a bad taste. Possibly,

---

[130] Mitter, 185.

Stilwell had planned to use his diary to tell his story someday. And surely, it would have been greatly cleaned up. But it wasn't, and the derogatory comments were often quoted with little context, painting Stilwell in a bad light. To say that the frankness of his reflections is unusual would be a massive understatement. A full general never would have approved the publication of his most private thoughts and frustrations. Today they are online in the Hoover Institution Library and Archives. Stilwell was tactful and careful in his press conference comments.

His words remain a frank, unremitting look at the difficult, almost tortured, experience he faced in China. Stilwell's unfiltered remarks are a classic study of the political pressures faced by American military commanders. He simultaneously had bosses from three countries. Even the instructions from the US were inconsistent as George Marshall and the joint chiefs tussled with Chiang/Chennault and FDR vacillated.

Stilwell bulldozed through the bureaucratic haze and phony niceties to speak truth to power. As he was developing plans for a North Africa assault in late 1941 (which he opposed), he wrote to his wife, "Besides being a rank amateur in all military matters, FDR is apt to act on sudden impulses. On top of that he has been completely hypnotized by the British, who have sold him a bill of goods." He was also critical that the Navy wasn't engaging the Japanese more quickly: "Maybe they took John Paul Jones's slogan seriously—'I have not yet begun to fight.'"

One undated diary entry from the second Burma campaign reads almost like a section from *Meditations* by Marcus Aurelius. "A good commander is a man of high character. This is the most important attribute, with power of decision the next most important attribute. He must have moral backbone, and this stems from high character; and he must be physically courageous." He said the average general envies the buck private. "The private carries the woes of one man; the general carries the woes of all." He even weighted the importance of the attributes of a good commander: character, 80 percent; power of decision, 10 percent; technical knowledge, 5 percent; and everything else, 5 percent. He admitted in his diary pre-Myitkyina that the four-month slog had dragged him down and that "he was nasty to people without any reason." Stilwell's poor technical knowledge of fast-improving airpower was a source of criticism.

It turned out that Chiang also kept a detailed diary. And amazingly, it's now stored at the same place as Stilwell's—the Hoover Library in California. In 2004, Elizabeth Chiang Fang Chih-yi, the widow of Chiang's grandson, began delivering his handwritten diaries—some badly damaged. They can be viewed and quoted under strict guidelines. His family felt his diary, although very personal at times, needed to be made public because of misunderstandings about Chiang. It's not clear to what extent either the Stilwell or Chiang diaries were redacted by family members. The Army also removed entries from Stilwell's diary.

Access to Chiang's view of events spawned a new academic assessment of the Chiang/Stilwell relationship in the last fifteen years, often with a more favorable view of Chiang and other Nationalists such as He Yingqin, Chiang's Commander in Chief. Many post-war American writers leaned heavily on Stilwell's diary and the writings of journalists sympathetic to Stilwell and failed to adequately investigate the Nationalist side. In the 2016 book titled *General He Yingqin: The Rise and Fall of Nationalist China*, Peter Worthing wrote, "While most American officials regarded He Yingqin as a die-hard reactionary, during the Chinese Civil War he proposed progressive economic reforms as the most effective way to counter the appeal of the Chinese communists." Worthing points out the Nationalist side. For example, he wrote, "While Stilwell fumed over what he perceived as Chinese failure to follow through on promises, He Yingqin also found that Stilwell did not always live up to his word."[131] Chiang and He engaged the Japanese in hard fighting before America entered the war, and adopted a more cautious approach after losing significant numbers of troops. Importantly, some modern Chinese writers such as Fan Jianchuan also look at Chiang Kai-shek in a more positive light.[132]

In the past three years, Chiang's memory has been under attack in Taiwan where young protesters have defaced and demanded removal of many of his statues. Efforts by Taiwanese authorities to portray

---

[131] Worthing, 214.
[132] Mitter, 183–185.

Chiang in a positive light have been rejected by a new generation who say they were brainwashed. The wisdom of Stilwell's Burma offensive strategy was questioned by some critics, while others noted how the Chinese were proud of the Second Burmese campaign. In an essay included in *The Battle for China*, Asano Toyomi wrote, "The Chinese victory over the Japanese in Burma became the most effective propaganda tool for the Nationalists not only to impress the world with the birth of the newly trained Chinese military equipped with modern weaponry, but also to argue that China had defeated Japan."[133]

Chinese soldiers in the fight to reopen the Burma Road. (Wikimedia Commons)

---

[133] Toyomi, 385.

The Chinese soldier won the war in northern Burma and southwestern China. The American contributions were leadership, training and equipping the Chinese armies, providing air and medical support, building the Ledo Road, and organizing Kachins into a valuable resource. The two long-range penetration forces were intended to provide an example to spur on Chinese commanders. The joint chiefs were extremely reluctant to divert any infantry to mainland Asia but felt compelled to provide the small provisional units to demonstrate American commitment to Chiang and Stilwell.

The British infantry played the decisive role in the victory at Imphal and a later invasion of central and southern Burma. Mountbatten was anointed first Earl Mountbatten of Burma in 1947.

American and Chiang's soldiers were in Burma to improve deliveries of trucks and other war materiel to Nationalist armies in China. America and China both strongly opposed returning Burma (or any colonies) to British rule. American rule of the Philippines was unwound by a congressional law passed in 1932.

Differing points of view of America's 1940s strategy in China could be debated. Would it have been easier to dislodge the Japanese from China than the Pacific Islands? Would Allied troops have been more effective in China than in North Africa?

The biggest question of all: What if FDR had overruled Chiang in 1944 and established Stilwell as the commander of all Chinese troops, Nationalist and Communist, responsible not to Chiang but to the US? Is it possible Mao could have become the stabilizing force and American ally that FDR had envisioned? Instead, in 1949 Mao had no choice but to turn to Stalin, who had dropped an Iron Curtain from the Baltic to the Adriatic. The cold war was on. Was there really any possibility of an alliance between the 1940s CCP and the United States? Whether Mao and his followers were even communists was questioned by Stalin. Stilwell, a Republican, had no interest in the Communist ideology; he respected them because they would fight.

There's no question that Stilwell's strategy and personality can be criticized. In retrospect, his China assignment was primarily political, not military. It was a job for which he was not suited, either in training or temperament. There was virtually no chance Chiang would have turned over his military to another commander. And Stilwell knew that in early 1942 when he said that he would serve his country as needed. Stilwell's attack mentality was part of an American military approach refined at Fort Benning by Marshall, who wanted no part of trench warfare. Stilwell first learned the approach under General John J. Pershing as he helped plan the American offensive at St. Mihiel in World War I. Some of Stilwell's critics err in writing as if it was his idea to aggressively push Chiang to fight. Stillwell was doing exactly what George Marshall and the US Joint Chiefs (via FDR) told him to do.

What *is* important today is how Stilwell is commemorated in Communist China. The Battle for Burma and the Burma Road are important examples of how Americans and Chinese worked together in a collaboration that is solemnly remembered.

ACKNOWLEDGMENTS

I used diaries, letters, and battle reports from actual participants whenever possible. No one directly involved made any record of what happened in the Standish attack, but a very thorough accounting was made by Edward Winslow of the Plymouth Plantation in a report sent to London investors. There were extensive records available from the other battles, some of which were collected. One example is John Moncure's excellent study on the Battle of Cowpens for the US Army Combat Studies Institute. Online access to diaries and other materials during the COVID-19 pandemic in 2020 to 2021 was invaluable.

I supplemented my research with well-known books, such as Barbara Tuchman's *Stilwell and the American Experience in China: 1911–1945* and Nathaniel Philbrick's *Mayflower: Voyage, Community, War*. Other books, such as Richard Dunlap's report on his personal experience with the OSS in Burma, provided great detail on the MARS Task Force that was not available in the official US Army history of the China-Burma-India Theater. My full bibliography is at the end of the book.

Walter Powell, a battlefield preservationist, founder of the Braddock Road Preservation Association and Pilgrim expert, reviewed and suggested additional resources for chapter 1, "Myles Standish and the Lost Colony," and chapter 2, "Young George Washington and Braddock's Defeat."

Robert T. Messner, a retired attorney and founder of Braddock's Battlefield History Center, reviewed and made comments on chapter 2, "Young George Washington and Braddock's Defeat."

Lawrence E. Babits, a professor at East Carolina University and author of *A Devil of a Whipping: The Battle of Cowpens*, reviewed and made several helpful suggestions on chapter 3, "Daniel Morgan and Cowpens."

Robert M. Dunkerly, National Park Service ranger, who has worked at Kings Mountain and studied Cowpens, reviewed and provided valuable comments on chapter 3, "Daniel Morgan and Cowpens."

Eugene Ware, an author and student of Erie, Pennsylvania, history, reviewed chapter 4, "Oliver Hazard Perry and the Battle of Lake Erie."

Brian Steel Wills, director of the Center for the Civil War Era and professor of history at Kennesaw State University, biographer of Nathan Bedford Forrest, and author of *The River Was Dyed with Blood: Nathan Bedford Forrest and Fort Pillow*, reviewed and made several valuable suggestions for chapter 5, "Nathan Bedford Forrest and the Fort Pillow Massacre."

Greg Mertz, a former National Park Service historian, read and provided comments for chapter 5, "Nathan Bedford Forrest and the Fort Pillow Massacre."

Michael Schaller, Regents professor of history at the University of Arizona and author of *The US Crusade in China 1938–1945*, read and commented on chapter 6, "'Vinegar Joe' Stilwell and the Battle for Burma."

Len Riedel, executive director of the Blue and Gray Education Society, assisted in connecting me with subject matter experts.

Kevin McCann, a student of history and literature and currently a French teacher at Randolph-Macon Academy in Front Royal, Virginia, read much of the manuscript and gave me valuable feedback on how to frame the concepts of remembrance.

Hal Jespersen, a professional cartographer and official cartographer for *Gettysburg Magazine*, produced ten custom maps.

Librarians
- Melissa Davis, director of library and archives, George C. Marshall Foundation, Lexington, Virginia
- Pamela Barroso, library assistant, Braddock Carnegie Library Association, Braddock, Pennsylvania
- The reference library staff at the Tufts Library, Weymouth, Massachusetts
- Lauren Chen, reference librarian, Leventhal Map Center, Boston Public Library
- Carlos Garcia-Minguillan, maps and manuscripts reference team, the British Library, London
- Terese Austin, reference librarian, William L. Clements Library, University of Michigan, Ann Arbor, Michigan
- Pearl McClintock and Jennifer Claybourne of the Upper Midwest Literary Archives at the University of Minnesota Libraries

I assume full personal responsibility for any errors.

BIBLIOGRAPHY

Chapter One: Myles Standish and the Lost Colony

Bunker, Nick. *Making Haste from Babylon.* New York: Vintage, 2011.
Dempsey, Jack. *Good News from New England and Other Writings on the Killings at Weymouth Colony.* Scituate, Massachusetts: Digital Scanning Inc., 2001
Donohue, Barbara. *Results of an Intensive (Locational) Survey at 43 Bicknell Road, Weymouth, Massachusetts.* Weymouth: The Weymouth Historical Commission, 2009.
Lord, G. Stinson, and Jack Frost. *Two Forts…to Destiny.* North Scituate, Massachusetts: Hawthorne Press, 1972.
Philbrick, Nathaniel. *Mayflower: Voyage, Community, War.* London: Penguin Books, 2007.
Pratt, Phineas. *A Declaration of the Affairs of the English People, That First Inhabited New England.* Boston, 1662.
Reséndez, Andrés. *The Other Slavery: The Uncovered Story of Indian Enslavement in America.* Boston: Houghton Mifflin Harcourt, 2016.
Silverman, David J. *This Land Is Their Land: The Wampanoags, Plymouth County, and the Troubled History of Thanksgiving.* New York: Bloomsbury Publishing, 2020.
Willison, George F. *Saints and Strangers.* New York: Time Life Books, 1981.
Winslow, Edward. *Good Newes from New England.* Bedford, Massachusetts: Applewood Books, first published in London in 1624.
Additional Sources:

Dempsey, Jack. "Keynote Address at Dedication of the Wessagusset/Weymouth Colony Site." Ancient Lights. July 11, 2004. http://ancientlights.org/weymouth.html.

Chen, Lauren. Winthrop maps. Leventhal Map Center, Boston Public Library, and Carlos Garcia-Minguillan, Maps and Manuscripts Reference Team, The British Library, London.

Chapter Two: Young George Washington and Braddock's Defeat

Alden, John Richard. *General Gage in America*. Baton Rouge, Louisiana: Louisiana State University Press, 1948.

Baker, Norman L. *Braddock's Road: Mapping the British Expedition from Alexandria to the Monongahela*. Charleston, South Carolina: The History Press, 2013.

Chernow, Ron. *Washington, a Life*. New York: The Penguin Press, 2010.

Franklin, Benjamin. *The Autobiography of Benjamin Franklin*. New Haven: Yale University Press, 2003.

Kopperman, Paul E. *Braddock at the Monongahela*. Pittsburgh: University of Pittsburgh Press, 1977.

Messner, Robert T. *Reflections from Braddock's Battlefield*. Braddock, Pennsylvania: Braddock's Field Historical Society, 2005.

Preston, David L. *Braddock's Defeat: The Battle of the Monongahela and the Road to Revolution*. Oxford, United Kingdom: Oxford University Press, 2015.

Winthrop, Sargent. *The History of an Expedition against Fort DuQuesne, in 1755: Under Major-General Edward Braddock*. Philadelphia: J. P. Lippincott and Co., 1856.

Schector, Barnett. *George Washington's America*. New York: Walker Publishing Co., 2010.

Stark, Peter. *Young Washington: How Wilderness and War Forged America's Founding Father*. New York: HarperCollins, 2018.

Zambone, Alfred Louis. *Daniel Morgan, a Revolutionary Life*. Yardley, Pennsylvania: Westholme Publishing, 2018.

Chapter Three: Daniel Morgan and Cowpens

Babits, Lawrence E. *A Devil of a Whipping: The Battle of Cowpens.* Chapel Hill, North Carolina: University of North Carolina Press, 2001.

Bearss, Edwin C. *Battle of Cowpens: A Documented Narrative and Troop Movement Maps.* Johnson City, Tennessee: Overmountain Press, 1996.

Buchanon, John. *The Road to Guilford Courthouse: The American Revolution in the Carolinas.* Hoboken, New Jersey: Wiley, 1999.

Davis, Burke. *The Cowpens-Guilford Courthouse Campaign.* Philadelphia and New York: J. P. Lippincott Co., 1962.

Greene, George, ed. *The Life of Nathanael Greene.* Carlisle, Massachusetts: Applewood Books, 2009.

Johnson, William. *Sketches of the Life and Correspondence of Nathanael Greene.* Self-published, 1821. Google Books.

Moncure, John. *The Cowpens Staff Ride and Battlefield Tour.* Fort Leavenworth, Kansas: US Army Combat Studies Institute, 1996.

Morgan, Richard L. *General Daniel Morgan: Reconsidered Hero.* Morgantown, North Carolina: Burke County Historical Society, 2001.

Patterson, Lee P. *Forgotten Patriot: The Life and Times of Major-General Nathanael Greene.* Irvine, California: Universal Publishers, 2002.

Pybus, Cassandra. *Epic Journeys of Freedom: Runaway Slaves of the American Revolution and Their Global Quest for Liberty.* Boston: Beacon Press, 2007.

Schama, Simon. *Rough Crossings: Britain the Slaves and the American Revolution.* New York: HarperCollins, 2006.

Tarleton, Banastre. *A History of the Campaigns of 1780 and 1781: In the Southern Provinces of North America.* London: Andesite Press, 2017.

Zambone, Alfred Louis. *Daniel Morgan, a Revolutionary Life.* Yardley, Pennsylvania: Westholme Publishing, 2018.

Chapter Four: Oliver Hazard Perry and The Battle of Lake Erie

Bates, Samuel P. *History of Erie County, Pennsylvania.* Chicago: Warner, Beers & Co., 1884.

Bell, Herbert. *History of Venango County, Pennsylvania: Its Past and Present.* Venango, Pennsylvania: Brown, Runk & Company, 1890. Google Books.

Berton, Pierre. *Flames Across the Border.* Boston: Little Brown, 1981.

Clark, William P. *Official History of the Militia and the National Guard of the State of Pennsylvania.* 3 vols. Philadelphia: C. J. Hendler, 1909.

Cooper, James Fenimore. *The History of the Navy of the United States of America.* London, United Kingdom: Forgotten Books, 1862.

Ennis, Daniel James. *Enter the Press-gang: Naval Impressment in Eighteenth-Century British Literature.* Newark, Delaware: University of Delaware Press, 2002. Google Books.

Knoll, Denys W. *Battle of Lake Erie: Building the Fleet in the Wilderness.* Washington, DC: Naval Historical Foundation, 1979.

Mahan, Alfred Thayer. *Sea Power in Its Relations to the War of 1812.* Cambridge, United Kingdom: Cambridge University Press, 2011.

Mackenzie, Alexander. *Commodore Oliver Hazard Perry: Famous American Naval Hero, Victor of the Battle of Lake Erie, His Life and Achievements.* New York: D. M. MacLellan Book Company, 1910. Google Books.

Mead, Spencer. *History and Genealogy of the Mead Family of Fairfield County, Connecticut, Eastern New York, Western Vermont, and Western Pennsylvania, from AD 1180 to 1900.* New York: Knickerbocker Press, 1901. Google Books.

Roosevelt, Theodore. *The Naval War of 1812: A Complete History.* Mineola, New York: Dover Publications, 2017.

Sanford, Laura. *The History of Erie County, Pennsylvania, from Its First Settlement.* Self-published. 1894.

Skaggs, David Curtis, and Larry L. Nelson. *Sixty Years' War for the Great Lakes, 1754–1814.* East Lansing, Michigan: Michigan State University Press.

Chapter Five: Nathan Bedford Forrest and the Massacre at Fort Pillow

Baptist, Edward E. *The Half Has Never Been Told.* New York: Basic Books, 2014.

Carroll, John W. *Autobiography and Reminiscences of John W. Carroll.* Electronic Edition. Academic Affairs Library, University of North Carolina at Chapel Hill, 1996. https://docsouth.unc.edu/fpn/carroll/carroll.xml.

Cimprich, John. *Fort Pillow, a Civil War Massacre, and Public Memory.* Baton Rouge: Louisiana State University Press, 2005.

Davison, Eddy W., and Daniel Foxx. *Nathan Bedford Forrest: In Search of the Enigma.* Gretna, Louisiana: Pelican Publishing, 2007.

Foote, Shelby. *The Civil War: A Narrative.* Vol. 3, *Red River to Appomattox.* New York: Random House, 1974.

Gorra, Michael. *The Saddest Words: William Faulkner's Civil War.* New York: Liveright Publishing, 2020.

Grant, Ulysses S. *Personal Memoirs of U. S. Grant.* 2 vols. New York: Charles L. Webster and Company, 1885–1886. ISBN 0-914427-67-9.

Levin, Kevin M. *Searching for Black Confederates: The Civil War's Most Persistent Myth.* Chapel Hill: The University of North Carolina Press, 2019.

Macaluso, Gregory J. *The Fort Pillow Massacre: The Reason Why.* New York: Vantage Press, 1989.

Sandburg, Carl. *Abraham Lincoln: The War Years.* New York: Harcourt Brace, 1939.

Sheehan-Dean, Aaron, ed. *The Civil War, the Final Year Told by Those Who Lived It.* New York: Library Classics of America, 2014.

Sherman, William T. *Memoirs of General W. T. Sherman.* Boone, Iowa: Library of America, 1990.

Simpson, Brooks D., ed. *The Civil War: The Final Year Told by Those Who Lived It.* 2013.

Smith, Clint. *How the Word Is Passed: A Reckoning with the History of Slavery Across America.* Boston: Little Brown and Company, 2021.

Varon, Elizabeth. *Armies of Deliverance, a New History of the Civil War.* New York: Oxford University Press, 2019.

Ward, Andrew. *River Run Red: The Fort Pillow Massacre in the American Civil War.* New York: Viking Adult, 2005.

Wills, Brian Steel. *The Confederacy's Greatest Cavalryman: Nathan Bedford Forrest.* Lawrence: University Press of Kansas, 1992.

Wills, Brian Steel. *The River Was Dyed with Blood: Nathan Bedford Forrest and Fort Pillow.* University of Oklahoma Press, 2014.

Charles River Editors. *The Fort Pillow Massacre: The History and Legacy of the Civil War's Most Notorious Battle.* Boston: CreateSpace Publishing, 2015.

Castel, Albert. "The Fort Pillow Massacre: A Fresh Examination of the Evidence," *Civil War History* 4, no. 1 (1958).

United States War Department. *The War of the Rebellion: A Compilation of the Official Records of the Union and Confederate Armies*, series 1, vol. 32, part 1. Washington: Government Printing Office, 1880–1901. https://babel.hathitrust.org/cgi/pt?id=coo.31924080787462&view=1up&seq=521&q1=Fort%20Pillow0/l.

Smith, Clint. "The War on Nostalgia." *The Atlantic*, June 2021.

Douglass, Frederick. "Black Soldiers in the US Military During the Civil War." National Archives. August 15, 2016. Retrieved January 5, 2021.

United States Colored Troops History. African American Civil War Museum. https://www.afroamcivilwar.org/about-us/usct-history.html.

US Congress Joint Committee on the Conduct of the War, "Fort Pillow Massacre." House Report No. 65, 38th Congress, 1st

Session. National Archives at College Park, College Park, Maryland. https://archive.org/details/fortpillowmassac00unit.

Senate Report 63, 38 Congress, 1 sess., Serial 1178; House of Representatives Report 65, 38 Congress, 1 sess., Serial 1278; and Letters Received from Executive Officers, compiled 1831–1869; General Records of the Department of Treasury, Record Group 56 National Archives at College Park, College Park, Maryland.

The Confederate Casualties of Battle of Fort Pillow. http://www.custermen.com/DixieBoys/FtPillowCSA.htm.

Hoole's Company, Mississippi Light Artillery, Regiment History. http://www.civilwardata.com/active/hdsquery.dll?RegimentHistory?2662&C.

The Battle of Fort Pillow. Official Records. https://civilwarhome.com/ftpillow.html.

Chapter Six: Vinegar Joe Stillwell and the Burma Road

Astor, Gerald. *The Jungle War: Mavericks, Marauders and Madmen in the China-Burma-India Theater of World War II*. Hoboken, New Jersey: J. Wiley & Sons, 2004.

Dallek, Robert. *Franklin D. Roosevelt and American Foreign Policy, 1932–1945*. Oxford, England: Oxford Paperbacks. 1995.

Dorn, Frank. *Walkout, with Stilwell in China*. New York: Thomas Y. Crowell Co., 1971.

Dunlop, Richard. *Behind Japanese Lines, with the OSS in Burma*. Chicago: Rand McNally, 1979.

Elegant, Robert S. *Mao vs. Chiang. The Battle for China, 1925–1949*. New York: Grosset and Dunlap, 1972.

Hahn, Emily. *Chiang Kai-shek, an Unauthorized Biography*. New York: Open Road Media, 2015.

Hunter, Charles N. *Galahad*. San Antonio, Texas: The Naylor Co., 1963.

Ichinokuchi, Tad, and Daniel Ausi. *John Aiso and the MIS Japanese-American Soldiers in the Military Intelligence Service, World War II*. Monterey, California: Military Intelligence Service, 1988.

Kurtz-Phelan, Daniel. *The China Mission: George Marshall's Unfinished War, 1945–1947*. New York: W. W. Norton Co., 2018

Latimer, Jon. *Burma: The Forgotten War*. London: John Murray, 2004.

Mitter, Rana. *Forgotten Ally: China's World War II, 1937–1945*. Boston: Houghton Mifflin Harcourt, 2013.

Nakahata, Yuraki. *Mars Task Force, Burma Campaign, Secret Valor: MIS Personnel World War II Pacific Theater*. Honolulu, Hawaii: Military Intelligence Service Veterans, 1993.

Peattie, Mark, Edward Drea, and Hans van der Ven, eds. *The Battle for China*. Stanford, California: Stanford University Press, 2011.

Randolph, John. *Marsmen in Burma*. Houston, Texas: John Randolph Publisher, 1946.

Romanus, Charles F., and Riley Sunderland. *Stiwell's Command Problems*. Washington, DC: US Army Center of Military History, 1987.

Romanus, Charles F., and Riley Sunderland. *US Army in World War II: The China-Burma-India Theater. Time Runs Out*. Washington, DC: Office of the Chief of Military History, United States Army, 1959.

Schaller, Michael. *The US Crusade in China, 1938–1945*. New York: Columbia University Press, 1979.

Taylor, Jay. *The Generalissimo: Chiang Kai-shek and the Struggle for Modern China*. Cambridge, Massachusetts: Belknap Press, 2011.

Tuchman, Barbara. *Practicing History*. New York: Alfred A. Knopf, 1981.

Tuchman, Barbara. *Stilwell and the American Experience in China, 1911–1945*. New York: Macmillan Publishers. 1971.

Van de Ven, Hans. *China at War: Triumph and Tragedy in the Emergence of the New China.* Cambridge, Massachusetts: Harvard University Press, 2017.

Webster, Donavan. *Burma Road: The Epic Story of the China-Burma-India Theater in World War II.* New York: Farrar, Strauss and Giriux, 2003.

Worthing, Peter. *General He Yingqin: The Rise and Fall of Nationalist China.* Cambridge, United Kingdom: Cambridge University Press, 2016.

Agarwall, Ritu. "TENGCHONG: A forgotten episode in northern theatre," *The Pioneer*, November 26, 2016. https://www.dailypioneer.com/2016/columnists/tengchong-a-forgotten-episode-in-northern-theatre.html.

Camina, Matthew James. "The Most Forgotten Unit in the Most Forgotten Battle of That War." Master's thesis, Texas A&M University, 2013.

Easterbrook, Ernest F. "The World War II Diaries of Ernest F. Easterbrook (1944–1945)." Hoover Institution online Archives. https://digitalcollections.hoover.org/internal/media/dispatcher/213268/full.

Nathan, Andrew. "An Anxious 100th Birthday for China's Communist Party: Can the Party Survive a Modernized China?" *Wall Street Journal*, June 27, 2021.

Perlez, Jane. "China Maintains Respect, and a Museum, for a US General." *The New York Times*, February 23, 2016.

Saquety, Troy. "Over the Hills and Far Away: The MARS Task Force, the Ultimate Model for Long Range Penetration Warfare." *Veritas, the Journal of Army Special Operations History* 5, no. 4 (2009). https://arsof-history.org/articles/v5n4_over_the_hills_page_1.html.

Stilwell, Joseph. The World War II Diaries of General Joseph W. Stilwell, (1941–1945). Hoover Institution Archives (online). https://digitalcollections.hoover.org/internal/media/dispatcher/213318/full.

"H. L. Boatner Papers." Accession number 90. George C. Marshall Research Foundation. Lexington, Virginia.

Papers and Minutes of Meetings. The Joint Staff. The Quadrant Conference. 1943. https://www.jcs.mil/Portals/36/Documents/History/WWII/Quadrant3.pdf.

Merrill's Marauders. "Pass in Review." http://www.marauder.org/passing.htm.

GENERAL SOURCES

LePore, Jill. *These Truths: A History of the United States.* New York: W. W. Norton & Company, 2019.

Nora, Pierre. *Realms of Memory.* New York: Columbia University Press, 1998.

INDEX

"The Hump" 133
124th Cavalry 150, 154, 156, 157, 163, 165, 174
475th Infantry Regiment 150
Abenaki (tribe) 4
Aberdikes (tribal chief) 6, 7, 10
abolitionists 66
Adams, Charles Francis Jr. 14
Adams, John 44
A Devil of a Whipping: The Battle of Cowpens 63
African American Civil War Museum 122
African Americans 65, 67, 116, 118
Alabama 94, 99, 119
Alden, John 11
Alden, John Richard 41
Alexander, Harold 130
Allegheny Mountains 21, 26, 27, 75
Allegheny River 30
American Battlefield Trust 19
American Experience (documentary) 11
Anaconda Plan 96
Anderson, Lee P. 49
Annapolis, Maryland 89
Armies of Deliverance: A New History of the Civil War 114

artillery 26, 61, 79, 104, 105, 106, 109, 110, 140, 151, 161, 162, 163, 164, 167, 170
Asano Toyomi 129, 144, 166, 182
Babits, Lawrence 54, 60, 63, 67, 69
Baker, Charlie 2
Baker, Norman L. 28
Baptist, Edward E. 120
Barclay, Robert Heriot (commander) 80, 82, 83, 84, 86
Battle of Grand Pré 30
Battle of Kings Mountain 48
Battle of the Crater 114
Battle of the Monongahela 19, 29, 34, 41, 67
Battle of the Teutoburg Forest 19
Battle of the Wabash River 44
Bearss, Ed (historian) 54, 59, 71
Beauregard, P. T. (general) 97
Berryville, Virginia 67
Berton, Pierre 91
Bicknell site 15
Black Loyalist Heritage Centre 66
Black Rock Naval Base 77

201

Blacks 65, 66, 95, 98, 99, 106, 112, 121, 122, 135
Boatner, Haydon L. 135, 136, 138, 143, 144, 146, 154
Book of Negroes 66
Boone, Daniel 26, 39
Booth, Lionel F. (major) 100, 101
Boston 3, 11, 12, 14, 41, 52, 80, 82, 117
Braddock at the Monongahela 28, 40
Braddock, Edward (general) 18, 24
Braddock, Pennsylvania 32, 43
Braddock Road 27, 28
Braddock Road Preservation Association (BRPA) 27
Braddock's Battlefield History Center 46
Braddock's Defeat (the battle) 19, 20, 43, 44
Braddock's Defeat (the book) 29
Braddock's Field 19, 40, 42, 46
Bradford, William 1, 6
Bradford, William T. 100
Bragg, Braxton (general) 98
brig-rigged corvettes 77
Britain 23, 69, 73, 74, 75, 89, 128, 129, 173
British Army (Regulars) 19, 20, 41, 65
British Museum 14
British Parliament 63, 69
Brockton, Massachusetts 12
Brooklyn Navy Yard 76, 77
Brown, John 120, 122
Buffalo, New York 77, 78

Burma (Myanmar) 129, 130, 133, 134, 135, 141, 142, 143, 146, 148, 151, 152, 153, 162, 166, 170, 173, 174, 178, 183
Burnside, Ambrose E. 114
Burns, Ken 115
Burns, Ric 11
Burton, Ralph (lieutenant colonel) 32, 34
Butler, Samuel 11
Cairo Conference 137
California 128, 129, 135, 140, 179, 181
Canada 29, 65, 73, 75, 76, 89, 91
Canadian Museum of History 33
canots du maître 33
Canton, Massachusetts 11
Carmel, California 179
Carnegie, Andrew 42, 45, 46
Carroll, John W. 107
carronades 79, 80, 82, 83, 85, 90
Case Western Reserve University 116
cavalry 47, 49, 54, 55, 56, 57, 59, 60, 61, 62, 68, 69, 71, 92, 95, 96, 97, 98, 99, 104, 106, 108, 115, 123, 150, 154, 156, 171, 173
CBI Roundup 131, 151, 166, 169, 175
Central Aircraft Manufacturing Corp. 129
Central Intelligence Agency (CIA) 135

Chalmers, James R. (brigadier general) 101, 103, 108, 109
Chancellorsville 114
Charles-Henri-Louis d'Arsac, chevalier de Ternay (Admiral Ternay) 50
Charles Michel Mouet de Langlade 29
Charleston, South Carolina 48, 50, 65, 72, 116, 118
Charlotte, North Carolina 48, 49, 83, 85, 86
Chattanooga, Tennessee 98, 100
Chauncey, Isaac 76, 77, 78, 79
Chennault, Claire 127, 128
Chiang Kai-shek (Jiang Jieshi) 125, 126, 132, 152, 176, 181
Chicago 76, 117, 156, 164
Chickamauga 99
Chickasaw 96
Chickataubut (tribal chief) 10
China 124, 125, 126, 127, 128, 129, 130, 132, 133, 134, 135, 136, 137, 138, 148, 152, 154, 156, 162, 168, 172, 176, 177, 180, 181, 182, 183, 184
China at War Triumph and Tragedy in the Emergence of the New China, 1937–1952 130
China-Burma-India (CBI) Theater 129
China's Good War How World War II Is Shaping a New Nationalism 179

Chindits 136, 138, 142, 144, 147, 171
Chinese Air Force 127
Chinese Army of India (Chih Hui Pu) 135
Chinese Communist Party (CCP) 125, 126, 127, 130, 134, 153, 172, 183
Chinese Expeditionary Force (CEF) 134, 135, 141, 154, 156, 157, 158, 162, 178
Cholmley, Robert (captain) 37
Chou En-lai (Zhou Enlai) 134, 152
Chungking (Chongqing), China 127, 128, 132, 152, 178
Churchill, Winston 136, 173
Cimprich, John 99, 106
civil rights movement 116
Civil War 19, 27, 92, 93, 95, 96, 114, 115, 116, 117, 121, 122, 139, 142, 171, 173, 181
Claude-Pierre Pécaudy de Contrecoeur 33
Clay, Henry 75
Clinton, Bill 90
Clinton, Henry 48, 63
Clinton, Hillary 90
Coates, Ta-Nehisi 115
Cochranton, Pennsylvania 91
Columbia, Tennessee 120
Combat Veteran Stories of World War II 145
Concord, Massachusetts 54
Confederate Army 97, 121
Confederate States (Confederacy) 95, 96, 97, 99, 101, 116, 119, 121, 122

Continental Army (Continentals) 41, 48, 55, 63
Continental Congress 49
Cooper, James Fennimore 87
Corbitant (tribal leader) 5
Corinth, Mississippi 97
Cornwallis, Charles (general) 48, 49, 50, 62, 63, 69
cotton 95, 120
Cowpens, Battle of 42, 47, 52, 53, 61
Craig Chartier 15
Crowninshield, Benjamin W. (Secretary of the Navy) 86
Cumberland, Maryland 26
Cumberland River 96
Custer, George Armstrong (general) 19, 173
Daughters of the Confederacy 116
Davies, John P. 134, 172
Davis, Jefferson 99, 120
de Beaujeu, Daniel Lienard (captain) 29
Delano, Warren Jr. 126
Delaware 55, 60, 75
Department 101 135, 137, 146, 155, 174
Dermer, Thomas 4
detention camps 140
Detroit 75, 76, 78, 79, 80, 82, 83, 85, 86, 88
Dewey, Thomas E. 153
Dinwiddie, Robert 20
Dixie Mission (US Army Observation Group) 152
Dobbins, Daniel 76, 77, 78
Donovan, William 134, 135, 146, 172

Dorn, Frank 130, 137, 141
Douglas C-47 Skytrain transports 149
Down Along with That Devil's Bones 119
Duke of Halifax 23
Dumas, Jean Daniel 35, 36
Dunbar's camp 42
Dunbar, Thomas (colonel) 28, 41, 42
Dunkerly, Robert M. 48, 61, 70
Dunkin Donuts 11
Dunmore's proclamation 63
Dutch 28
Easterbrook, Ernest F. (colonel) 157, 158, 162, 164, 165
Edgar Thomson (ET) Works 45
Eldridge, Fred 131, 175
Elliot, Jesse (lieutenant) 77, 79, 86
Elliott, Jesse (lieutenant) 82, 85, 86, 87
Emancipation Proclamation 99
Epic Journeys of Freedom: Runaway Slaves of the American Revolution and Their Global Quest for Liberty 65
Erie Maritime Museum 90
Erie, Pennsylvania 30
Ethiopian Regiment 63
Faulkner, William 93, 110, 114
Fawcett, Tom 40
Fifty-Fourth Massachusetts Regiment 118
First Virginia Ranger Company 39
Fitch, Charles 109
Flames Across the Border

The Canadian-American Tragedy, 1813–1814 91
Flying Tigers 129, 151, 174
Foote, Andrew H. 96
Foote, Shelby 93, 98, 114, 115
Forbes, John (general) 20
Fore River 14, 15
Forgotten Patriot: The Life and Times of Major-General Nathanael Greene 49
Forks of the Ohio 19, 20, 21, 31
Forrest, Nathan Bedford 68, 92, 93, 94, 101, 115, 119, 121
Fort de la Presqu'île 20, 33
Fort de la Rivière au Bœuf (or LeBoeuf) 20
Fort Donelson 96, 97, 98
Fort Duquesne 22, 26, 28, 29, 30, 31, 33, 35, 40
Fort Erie 89
Fort Henry 96
Fort Ligonier 46
Fort Machault 20
Fort Malden 78, 80
Fort Michilimackinac 29
Fort Necessity 22, 23, 28, 43, 44, 46
Fort Niagara 30
Fort Pillow 92, 93, 95, 97, 98, 99, 100, 106, 107, 108, 110, 111, 112, 113, 114, 115, 121, 122
Fort Pitt 63
Fort Riley, Kansas 150, 156, 165, 171, 173, 174
Forty-Eighth Regiment of Foot 40
Foundry United Methodist Church 90
Fox 28
Foxall, George 79
France 23
Franklin, Benjamin 18, 19, 20, 25
Fraser, John 21
fratricide 20, 37, 38, 40
Frederick, Maryland 25
Fredericksburg 114
French and Indian War 19, 20, 28, 46, 156
French Canadian Marines 19
French Creek 30
French, Daniel Chester 2
French Indochina 128
Gage, Thomas (lieutenant colonel) 32, 34, 37, 41
Gates, Horatio (captain) 35, 41, 48, 49, 50
Gauss, Clarence E. 138
General Gage in America 41
General Henry Dearborn 76
General He Yingqin The Rise and Fall of Nationalist China 181
General Society of *Mayflower* Descendants 11
Genzo, Minakami 146
George II (English king) 20
Georgia 48, 54, 55, 65, 71, 72, 117, 118, 119
Georgia Refugees 71
Gettysburg, Pennsylvania 13, 19
Gila River Indian Reservation 151
Giovanni da Verrazzano 4
Gist, Christopher 21

Good Newes From New England 10
Gorges, Ferdinando 4
Gorra, Michael 93, 110
Grant, Ulysses S. 97, 111, 139
Great Lakes 28, 31, 77, 78
Great Meadows 22, 28, 40
Great White Fleet 88
Green Bay, Wisconsin 29
Green, Brenda "Ren" 12
Greene, Nathanael 49, 54
Green, Thomas 12, 17
grenadier 19, 34
Griswold, Stanley (colonel) 144
Guilford Courthouse 62
gunboats 77, 78, 80, 82, 96, 98
Halkett, Peter 34, 40
Hamilton, Paul 76
Harrison, William Henry 76
He Yingqin 152, 181
Hingham Bay 14
Historical Society of Pennsylvania 24
History of Erie County, Pennsylvania 77, 91
History of the Campaigns of 1780 and 1781 59, 63
HMS *Detroit* 80
HMS *Guerriere* 82
Hobbamock (tribal warrior) 3
Homestead, Pennsylvania 46
Hooker, Joseph 114
Hopkins, Stephen 5
House of Representatives 67, 75
House of Skulls 15, 17
Houston, Texas 158, 174
Howard, John Eager (lieutenant colonel) 55, 58, 60, 61, 70
Hudibras (poem) 11
Hudson, Ohio 122
Huffine, Fred 142, 143, 146
Hull, Cordell 138
Hundred Regiments Offensive 128
Hunter, Charles 140
Hunt's Hill 15
Hunt, Thomas 4
Hyde Park, New York 126
Illinois 89, 151
Imphal, India 141, 166
impressment 74
indentured servants 41
Indiana 44, 76, 89
Iroquois 21, 28
Island Number Ten 98
Jackson, Andrew 73, 119
Jackson, Thomas J. "Stonewall" 95, 114, 117
Jamestown 4, 5
Japan 126, 127, 128, 129, 137, 140, 151, 166, 182
Japanese Americans 140, 151, 174
Jefferson, Thomas 74
Johnson, Albert Sidney 116
Johnson, Andrew 112, 119
Joseph Coulon de Villiers, Sieur de Jumonville 22
Jumonville 22, 23, 27, 38, 44, 45
Kachins 155, 183
Kansas 147, 150, 156, 165, 171, 173, 174
Kemter, Barnard 122
Kendle, Wesley D. 150
Kentucky 75, 96, 100
Khrushchev, Nikita 172
King Philip's War 11

Knight, Jack L. 163, 173
Knoll, Denys W. 79, 80, 89
Knox, Henry 50
Komoto, Kazuo "Kaz" (sergeant) 151
Kooperman, Paul E. 28, 40
Korea 172
Ku Klux Klan 69, 95, 112, 115, 119
Kunming, China 136, 138, 154, 168, 170
Lake Erie 20, 30, 73, 74, 76, 77, 78, 79, 80, 82, 87, 88, 90, 91
Lake Huron 29
Lake Ontario 30, 76
Lake Superior 29
Landis, Robert W. 149
Langdon, William R. 138
La Salle (French explorer) 20
Lashio, Burma (Myanmar) 128, 147, 158, 167, 169
Lattin, John H. 158, 164
Lawrence 77, 79, 80, 82, 85, 88, 90
Lawrence, James (captain) 80
Leaming, Mack J. (lieutenant) 104, 105, 106, 107, 108
Ledo Road (Stilwell Road) 133, 140, 144, 154, 155, 162, 168, 169, 172, 179, 183
Lee, Charles (lieutenant) 41
Lee, Robert E. 95, 114, 117
Lend-Lease 128, 129, 153
Leslie, Alexander (major general) 50
Lexington, Virginia 136, 143, 144, 145, 153, 169
Library of Congress 81

Lincoln, Abraham 3, 95, 99, 117
Lincoln, Benjamin (general) 48
Little Bighorn 19
Liverpool, England 66, 69
Lo Cho-Ying 136
Lockheed P-38 Lightning 140
Loi-kang Ridge 158, 159, 160, 163, 164
Longfellow, Henry Wadsworth 1, 2, 11
Long March 127, 171
Lord, G. Stinson 15
Lost Cause 95, 97, 116, 117
Louisiana 106
Louis XV (French king) 20
Lowell, Massachusetts 120
Loyalists 48, 51, 66
Lungling (Longling) 141
Lyons, Fred O. (captain) 144
Macaluso, Gregory (historian) 100
MacArthur, Douglas 172, 174, 177
Madison, James 75, 76
Magnes, Mary 46
Mahan, Alfred Thayer (historian) 85, 87
Maine 4, 10
Manuel, Herman 150
Mao Tse-tung (Mao Zedong) 125, 152
Marshal Jean-Baptiste Donatien de Vimeur, comte de Rochambeau (Count Rochambeau) 50
Marshall, George C. 117, 125, 143, 144, 145, 153, 169
Marshall, John 47

Marsmen in Burma 158, 162, 174
Mars Task Force (MTF or US Army 5,332nd Brigade) 150, 151, 154, 155, 156, 162, 164, 167, 168, 169, 170, 171, 173, 174, 175
Maruyama, Husayaso 144
Maryland 24, 25, 55, 60, 89
Mashpee Wampanoag (tribe) 5
Massachusett-Ponkapoag Tribal Council 13
Massachusetts Bay Colony 3, 9, 14
Massachusett tribe 3, 11, 12, 13, 17
Massasoit Ousamequin (tribal chief) 5
Matsumoto, Roy (sergeant) 140, 173
Mayflower 1, 4, 6, 8, 11
McCarthy, Joseph (senator) 172
McJunkin, Joseph (major) 62
McKeesport, Pennsylvania 40, 46
McMichael, Scott R. (colonel) 143
Mead, David (general) 75, 79, 80, 81, 89
Medal of Honor 95, 163
Memphis, Tennessee 93, 95, 96, 97, 98, 105, 119, 120, 123
Merchant Adventurers 5
Merrill, Frank 138
Merrill's Marauders (5,307th Composite Unit or Galahad) 138, 140, 142, 145, 146, 147, 149, 150, 151, 164, 165, 171, 173

Mertz, Greg 114, 115, 118
Messner, Robert 19, 40, 43, 44, 45, 46
Metacom (tribal chief) 11
Mexican War 96
Mexico 174
Miami 28
Michel-Ange Duquesne de Menneville (governor-general) 20
Michigan 28
militia 8, 10, 11, 21, 22, 24, 33, 34, 35, 47, 48, 50, 54, 58, 60, 61, 62, 67, 69, 70, 71, 75, 79, 80, 81, 91
Mineral Wells, Texas 173
Minnesota 108
Mississippi River 95, 96, 98, 105, 109, 123
Missouri 96, 101, 140, 149, 170, 174
Missouri Muleskinners' Society 174
Moncure, John (lieutenant colonel) 47, 48
Moncure, John (liutenant colonel) 70
Monmouth, New Jersey 48
Monongahela River 32, 34, 36, 39, 43
Montreal 19, 30, 33
Moraviantown, Ontario 88
Morgan, Daniel 26, 41, 47, 50, 51, 55, 70, 139
Morton, Thomas 10
Moswetuset Hummock (tribal site) 13

Mountbatten, Louis 136, 145, 153, 167, 173, 178, 179, 183
mules 140, 149, 156, 159, 170, 171
Mumford, James (corporal) 81
Murch, Richard 145
Murray, John (Lord Dunmore) 63
Museum of the Civil War 117
musket 7, 104
Myitkyina, Burma (Myanmar) 133, 134, 135, 139, 142, 143, 144, 145, 146, 147, 148, 149, 150, 153, 154, 155, 162, 178, 180
My Lai massacre 95
Namasket (village) 5
Namhkam, Burma (Myanmar) 141, 169
Nanking (Nanjing), China 127, 177
Napoleon 89
Napoleonic Wars 75
Narragansett (tribe) 4, 5
Nash, Gary 63
Nashville, Tennessee 95
National Confederate Museum 120
Nationalist (Kuomintang or KMT) 125
National Park Service (NPS) 19, 46, 59, 61, 72, 90, 114, 122, 174
National Rifle Association's Firearms Museum 11
Native Americans 4, 16, 18, 19, 21, 22, 26, 28, 33, 35, 44, 45, 52, 67, 75, 76, 89, 95

Naval Historical Foundation 79
Nelson, Horatio (vice admiral) 84
Nemacolin's Path 26
New England 6, 73, 75
New France 20, 23, 30
New Market 117
New Orleans 31, 73, 97
New York 24, 47, 48, 53, 65, 76, 120, 126
New York City 47, 120
New York Times 122, 153
Niagara 77, 79, 80, 82, 85, 90
Niagara Falls 30, 31
North Braddock, Pennsylvania 32
North Carolina 24, 35, 48, 50, 55, 62, 69, 71, 118, 173, 175
Northern Combat Area Command (NCAC) 138
North Weymouth, Massachusetts 3
Nova Scotia 30, 66
Octabiest (tribal chief) 10
Office of Strategic Services (OSS) 134
Ohio 28, 29, 44, 52, 73, 74, 76, 82, 88, 90, 116, 122, 149, 171
Ohio River 19
Ohio Valley 67
Ojibwa 35
O'Neil, Conner Towne 119
Ontario 33, 78, 88
Operation Ichigo 151
Orme, Robert (brevet captain) 34, 36, 37, 41
Ottawa 28, 29, 35

P-40 fighters 128
Patuxet (tribal village) 4, 5, 13, 16
Pearl Harbor 129, 135
Pecksuot (tribal warrior) 3, 4, 7, 9, 10, 15
Peking (Beijing) 127
Pennsylvania 18, 22, 24, 30, 32, 40, 42, 43, 50, 52, 67, 75, 90, 149, 171
Pennsylvania Gazette 41
Pennsylvania Railroad 40
People's Liberation Army (PLA) 128
Perry, Oliver Hazard 73, 74, 78, 82, 88, 90
Petersburg, Virginia 114
Peterson Cemetery 91
Peters, Paula 5, 11
Philadelphia 41, 49, 50, 79
Philbrick, Nathaniel 4
Pickens, Andrew (colonel) 51, 55, 58, 61, 62, 71
Pilgrims 3, 4, 5, 6, 7, 10
Pillow, Gideon Johnson (general) 98
Pittsburgh 19, 23, 31, 40, 63, 79
Pittsburg Landing 97
Pitt, William 23
Plimoth Patuxet 13
Plymouth Archaeological Rediscovery Project 15
Plymouth Plantation 1, 3, 5, 10, 11, 13
Plymouth Rock Foundation 6
Polk, James 119
Ponkapoag (reservation) 11, 12, 13
Potawatomi 35
Powell, Walter 13
Pratt, Phineas 6, 13, 15
press gangs 75
Preston, David 29, 34, 38, 45
Procter, Henry (major general) 88
Provincetown, Massachusetts 4, 5
Puma 150
Purdy, Jodi 17
Put-in-Bay, Ohio 73, 74, 90
Pybus, Cassandra 65, 66
Quebec 33, 52, 136, 138
Quebec Conference 138
Quincy, Massachusetts 13
Ramgarh, India 133
Randolph, John 158, 162, 167, 174, 175
Rangoon (Yangon) 129, 130, 133, 135, 158, 162, 165
Ranney, William 64
Reflections from Braddock's Battlefield 43
Republicans 112
Revolutionary War 41, 46, 47, 63, 66, 75
Rhode Island 4, 49, 78, 89, 120
River Run Red 110
Robinson, Charles 108
Robinson, John 3
Rome, Georgia 119
Roosevelt, Franklin D. 124, 125, 126, 128, 129, 134, 136, 137, 138, 152, 153, 172, 180, 183, 184
Roosevelt, Theodore 87
Rutledge, John 50
Sackets Harbor 76, 79

Saint-Gaudens, Augustus 118
Salisbury, North Carolina 50
Salween River 134
Sanders, John 17
San Francisco 45
Saratoga, New York 48, 52, 69
Sargent, Winthrop 24, 29
Savannah, Georgia 48
Schweibold, Jack (corporal) 171
Scribner, Vaughn (historian) 67
Searching for Black Confederates The Civil War's Most Persistent Myth 121
Second US Colored Light Artillery 100
Selma, Alabama 94, 119
Seneca 30
Seven Nations of Canada 35
Seventy-Fifth Army Ranger Regiment 173
Shakespeare 55
Shanghai, China 127, 170
Shaw, Robert Gould 118
Sherman, William T. 97, 100
Shiloh 97, 116, 118
Shirley, William (governor) 41
Sierra Leone 66
Signal Corps 155, 168
Singapore 128, 139, 166
Sino-Japanese War 128, 176
Sioux 28
Sixteenth Pennsylvania Militia 75
Sixth US Colored Heavy Artillery 100
Skaggs, David Curtis (historian) 87
slavery 4, 62, 63, 65, 66, 95, 99, 114, 115, 116, 117, 120
slaves 4, 45, 62, 63, 65, 66, 67, 95, 96, 98, 99, 100, 111, 112, 120, 121, 122
Smalls, Robert 115
Smith, Andrew Jackson 115
Smith, John (captain) 4
Smock, William 149, 156, 157, 159, 171
Soldier's Rest 67
Songshan Mountain 142
Sons of Confederate Veterans 120
South Carolina 23, 24, 35, 39, 47, 48, 50, 52, 54, 55, 65, 67, 69, 71, 72, 116, 119
South Carolina Independent Company 39
South East Asia Command (SEAC) 136
Southern Poverty Law Center 118
Soviet Union 127, 128, 137, 176
Spartanburg, South Carolina 67
Springfield rifle 136
Squanto (tribal warrior) 4, 5
Standish, Myles 1, 2, 4, 7, 10, 17
Standish. Myles 13
Stanton, Edwin 104
Stark, Peter 23
Staunton, Virginia 117
St. Clair, John (lieutenant colonel) 26
Stilwell and the American Experience in China: 1911– 1945 139
Stilwell, Joseph W. 124, 132, 177

Stilwell Road Museum 178
Stimson, Henry L. 129
St. Lawrence Valley 28
Stone Mountain 117, 119
Streight, Abel 99
Swails, Stephen 118
Taierzhuang, China 128, 179
Taiwan 172, 181
Tanaghrisson (Half King) 21
Tarleton, Banastre (colonel) 48, 53, 54, 55, 57, 58, 59, 60, 61, 62, 63, 64, 66, 68, 69, 70, 71
Tate, Edmund 51, 55, 60
Tecumseh (tribal leader) 75, 88, 89
Tengchung (Tengchong) 141
Tennessee Heritage Protection Act 119
Tennessee River 97
Tenth Air Force 147, 151
Texas 101, 140, 150, 158, 173, 174
The Case for the Defence of Banastre Tarleton A British assessment of Lt. Colonel Banastre Tarleton in the American War of Independence 68
The Generalissimo 137
The Half Has Never Been Told 96, 120
The History of an Expedition Against Fort DuQuesne, in 1755: Under Major-General Edward Braddock 24

The Lost Cause: A New Southern History of the War of the Confederates 116
The Naval War of 1812 87
The New English Canaan 10
The Patriot 68
The Saddest Words: William Faulkner's Civil War William Faulkner's Civil War 93
The Stilwell Papers 179
Thirteenth Tennessee Cavalry 100
Thrailkill, Benjamin F. (Frank) Jr. (colonel) 158, 163
Time Runs Out in CBI 157, 162
tobacco 96
Tokyo Rose 140
Tracing the Steps of General Stilwell 177
Trafalgar 80
Treaty of Ghent 89
Treaty of Old Town 96
Treaty of Paris 63
Trenton, New Jersey 48
Triplett, Francis 60
Truman, Harry 172
Trump, Donald J. 91
Tubman, Harriett 115
Tuchman, Barbara 132, 139, 152
Unger, William H. 151
Union Army 95, 97, 98, 99, 121
United States Colored Troops (USCT) 99, 122
University of Massachusetts–Boston 13
US Army 47, 48, 53, 70, 100, 114, 125, 138, 141, 143,

147, 148, 150, 151, 152, 157, 161, 162, 164, 175
US Army Combat Studies Institute 47, 48, 54
US Army Command and General Staff College 70, 147
US Joint Chiefs 130, 136
US Military Intelligence Service (MIS) 140
US Militia Act 99
US Naval Academy 89
USS *Constitution* 82
Valley Forge 48
van de Ven, Hans 128, 130, 151
Van Horn, Daniel 101, 108, 122
Van Leuven, Harry L. (private) 171
Varon, Elizabeth R. 114
Vicksburg National Military Park 118
Virginia 5, 11, 20, 22, 24, 27, 35, 38, 41, 44, 47, 49, 50, 51, 52, 55, 60, 63, 67, 91, 114, 117, 118
Virginia Legislature 63
Virginia Military Institute 117
von Steuben, Friedrich 48
Waggoner, Edmond (captain) 38
Walkout, with Stilwell In China 137
Wanting (Wanding) 141
Ward, Andrew 110
Ware, Eugene 77
War of 1812 73, 74, 75, 85, 87, 89, 90, 91
Washington 140, 171
Washington, DC 76, 79, 90, 122, 148, 152, 157, 161, 174
Washington, George 18, 19, 21, 34, 42, 43, 45, 46, 48, 52, 65, 91
Washington, Harry 66
Washington, Lawrence 21
Washington, William (lieutenant colonel) 51, 55, 64
Waterford, Pennsylvania 33
Waxhaws, South Carolina 48
Wedemeyer, Albert 153, 154
Wei Lihuang (Chinese commander) 141
Wessaguscus 14
Wessagusset (English trading colony) 6, 7, 13, 17
West, Donald J. 171
Weston Colony 6, 7, 9, 10, 11, 13, 14, 15, 16, 17
Weston, Thomas 3, 4
West Point 47, 54, 63, 96, 127
West Yunnan Anti-Japanese War Museum 177
Weymouth, George 4
Weymouth Historical Commission 15
Weymouth Public Library 12
Weymouth town meeting 17
Whiskey Rebellion 42, 67
White, Theodore 139, 144
Whitlow, Wright 121
Wilberforce, William 66
Willey, John P. 154, 157, 162, 169
Wills, Brian Steel 94, 98, 100, 105, 112, 113
Wingate, Orde 136, 171

Wins, Cedric T. (major general) 117
Winslow, Edward 7
Winthrop, John (governor) 9, 14
Wisconsin Historical Society 29
Wituwamat (tribal warrior) 3, 4, 8, 9, 10, 11, 13
World War II 124, 127, 133, 145, 148, 149, 151, 161, 171, 174, 175, 176, 178, 179
Wright, Aaron (sergeant) 81
Wyatt-Brown, Bertram 116
Wyoming 150
X-Force 132, 135, 141, 142, 147, 154, 162, 178
Yale 120
Yamakaze Detachment 160
Y-Force 132, 134, 136, 141, 142, 148, 153, 154, 178
Yunnan Province, China 128, 129, 132, 134, 135, 141, 154, 177, 178
Z-Force 133

ABOUT THE AUTHOR

Doug Smock is a retired newspaper reporter and magazine editor who lives in North Weymouth, Massachusetts. He co-authored two books on supply chain management, and now focuses on American history and remembrance through articles, lectures, and books.

CPSIA information can be obtained
at www.ICGtesting.com
Printed in the USA
BVHW021304221122
652524BV00023B/789